THE NORTH AFRICAN PROVINCES
FROM DIOCLETIAN TO THE
VANDAL CONQUEST

THE NORTH AFRICAN PROVINCES FROM DIOCLETIAN TO THE VANDAL CONQUEST

BY

B. H. WARMINGTON

Lecturer in Ancient History in the
University of Bristol

GREENWOOD PRESS, PUBLISHERS
WESTPORT, CONNECTICUT

Originally published in 1954 by the University Press,
Cambridge.

Reprinted with the permission of Cambridge University
Press.

Reprinted in 1971 by Greenwood Press,
a division of Congressional Information Service, Inc.
51 Riverside Avenue, Westport, Connecticut 06880

Library of Congress catalog card number 78-135615
ISBN 0-8371-5202-X

Printed in the United States of America

10 9 8 7 6 5 4 3 2

PREFACE TO THE REPRINT EDITION

This little book was written some twenty years ago when I was a postgraduate. Since that time so much work has been done on the history and archaeology of North Africa that it would take a very different form if rewritten today. However, since it seems that it is still of some interest and use, it is reprinted in its original form. I have taken the opportunity of adding to the bibliography a select number of books about, or referring to, Roman North Africa which have appeared since the first printing.

B.H.W.

BRISTOL
26 *February* 1970

PREFACE

This book is the substance of the Thirwall Prize Essay for 1951. I have to express my thanks to Mr J. Stevenson, Fellow of Downing College, Cambridge, for his guidance, and to the adjudicators and assessors of the Thirwall Prize for their comments which have, I hope, enabled me to avoid many errors.

B. H. W.

BRISTOL
12 *January* 1954

CONTENTS

LIST OF MAPS

ABBREVIATIONS

AE   *Année épigraphique.*

RAC   *Bulletin archéologique du Comité des travaux historiques et scientifiques.*

BSR   *Papers of the British School at Rome.*

C   *Corpus inscriptionum latinarum,* vol. VIII (Africa).

CIL   *Corpus inscriptionum latinarum,* other volumes.

CRAI   *Comptes rendus de l'Académie des inscriptions.*

CSEL   *Corpus scriptorum ecclesiasticorum latinorum.*

ILA   *Inscriptions latines d'Afrique.*

ILAlg   *Inscriptions latines de l'Algérie* (Gsell).

ILCV   *Inscriptiones latinae christianae veteres* (Diehl).

ILS   *Inscriptiones latinae selectae* (Dessau).

ILT   *Inscriptions latines de la Tunisie* (Merlin).

JRS   *Journal of Roman Studies.*

MGH   *Monumenta Germaniae historica.*

PIR   *Prosopographia imperii romani.*

PL   *Patrologiae cursus, series latina,* ed. Migne.

P-W   *Pauly-Wissowa, Real-Enzyklopädie der klassischen Altertumswissenschaft.*

SHA   Scriptores Historiae Augustae.

CHAPTER I

PROVINCIAL ADMINISTRATION IN AFRICA

O NE of the principal features of the administrative changes in the Empire at the end of the third century was the division of the existing provinces into smaller units by Diocletian. The history of the African provinces between 284 and 312 seems to show that there the changes were carried out in stages. At the beginning of Diocletian's reign, before 293,[1] the eastern and more settled part of Mauretania Caesariensis was made into a separate province having the name of Mauretania Sitifensis after its capital city, the *colonia* Sitifis. After 294, but perhaps in the years immediately following,[2] a new province, Byzacena, was created out of the southern part of Africa Proconsularis. About the same time Africa Proconsularis received part of the former Numidian province, including the substantial city of Theveste.[3] The earliest date for a separate province of Tripolitania, the interior of which had formerly been the responsibility of the legate of the Legio III Augusta, the coastal area of a legate of the proconsul, is from the reign of Maxentius (307–12);[4] but it seems more likely that the division took place under the Tetrarchy.[5] Numidia itself was divided into two provinces for a short while, the coastal area and the chief cities being in Numidia Cirtensis,[6] the southern frontier region being called Numidia Militiana.[7] The division may be dated to about

---

[1] *C* 8924, before the elevation of Galerius and Constantius.

[2] In 294, Africa Proconsularis was still undivided, but the governor at that date seems to have paid special attention to the restoration of cities in that part soon to be a separate province (see below, p. 31). The earliest record of the new province is in *ILAlg* 3832, between 295 and 305.

[3] See Ruinart, *Acta Sincera*, 309 f., for Theveste in Africa Proconsularis in 295.

[4] *AE* (1946), 149.

[5] *C* 22763 indicates that Aurelius Quintianus, *praeses* of Tripolitania, who had been *praeses* of Numidia in 303, completed a *centenarium* begun by Valerius Vibianus, *v.p.*, to be identified with the *praeses* of Tripolitania mentioned in *AE* (1929), 4. These can hardly be from the reign of Maxentius, who was in control of Africa only in 307/8 and 311/12, and it seems more likely that Aurelius Quintianus went from his Numidian position to Tripolitania than that he returned to Africa after some ten years.

[6] *C* 5526 (Thibilis, 306), *C* 7965 (Rusicade, 306).

[7] *C* 2345–7 (Thamugadi, 303–5).

305;[1] it was short-lived, for by 315 the province was united on its former basis, save that the capital was transferred from the military centre of Lambaesis to the chief city of the province, Cirta, a move which doubtless reflected the loss of military powers by the provincial governor.[2]

As in the early Empire, the highest in rank of these provinces was Africa Proconsularis; there were only two other provinces of this status, Achaia and Asia. The proconsulate had now no connexion with the position of consul which was reserved as a mark of the highest favour; those who held the proconsulate of Africa in the fourth century were frequently only at the beginning of their careers. Administratively, they were in most matters independent of the vicar of their diocese, and subordinate directly to the emperor. The distinctive position of these three provinces owed much to tradition—they had been proconsular provinces for centuries. Owing to their complete security they had no military importance, and so they served during the fourth century as a means whereby members of the senatorial aristocracy, excluded by policy or law from important military positions, could be launched on their careers.[3] The proconsulship of Africa was the first post in the long career of Sex. Petronius Probus (*procos. Afr.* 358), the second in that of Q. Clodius Hermogenianus Olybrius (*procos. Afr.* 361/2). Probus was perhaps the most powerful individual in the Empire under Valentinian, and Olybrius was likewise an important figure. Other proconsuls reached the rank of consul, praetorian prefect, or prefect of the city—an office traditionally reserved for the Roman nobility. Members of the powerful families of the Anicii and their close connexions, the Probi, and of the Ceionii, appear as proconsuls of Africa several times during the course of the century. In the period when Gratian was under the influence of Ausonius and honouring his former tutor with the highest positions, the poet's son Decimius Hesperius, and son-in-law Thalassius followed each other as proconsuls in 376/7 and 378 respectively.

[1] Valerius Florus, governor of Numidia Militiana mentioned in the inscription in the previous note, is found on an inscription from this part of Numidia, dated 303, with no note of its division (*AE* (1942), 8). It therefore occurred in his governorship.

[2] For other discussions of the dating of the reorganization, see, for example, Cagnat, in *Philologie et linguistique-mélanges à L. Havet*, and Seston, *Dioclétien et la Tétrarchie*, I, 326 ff.

[3] Pallu de Lessert, *Fastes des provinces africaines*, II, lists those after the accession of Diocletian.

Little less impressive is the list of governors of Numidia. In 320 this province was raised from praesidal to consular rank and in 362/3 received the unique title of 'sexfascalis'.[1] Four of its governors were from the family of the Ceionii; Vulcacius Rufinus, a relative of Julian, governed the province about 340, and Celsinus Adelfius, who married into the family of the Probi, between 333 and 337.[2] Byzacena, though it became a province of consular rank fairly early in the century, did not have such distinguished governors. Few of those who governed the Mauretanias (all of praesidal rank) are recorded; and while a fair number of *praesides* of Tripolitania are mentioned on inscriptions, their earlier and later careers remain almost completely unknown..

The chief duty of the provincial governor was judicial. He had competence over all civil and criminal cases except those in which privileged persons were involved, and minor offences left to the municipal magistrates. He was responsible also for seeing that all taxes were duly collected, and for ensuring the carrying out of public burdens by such people as the *curiales* and *navicularii*.

North Africa (except for Mauretania Tingitana) formed one of the dioceses created by Diocletian as an intermediate stage between the provinces and the prefectures; though the vicars of the dioceses were responsible not to the praetorian prefects but to the emperor. With a few short interruptions, the diocese of Africa was part of the praefecture comprising Illyria, Italy and Africa. The vicar of the diocese had little disciplinary power over the governors. Appeals from them (except from the proconsul of Africa) went to his court; and in the African diocese he had the additional task of supervising the collection of the food supplies for the city of Rome. The vicariate of Africa, though lower in rank than the proconsulate, was likewise held by many persons of wealth and nobility, including the brother and a cousin of Symmachus and one of the Probi.[3] The inclusion of Mauretania Tingitana in the diocese of Spain was due to the difficulty of communication between it and the rest of Roman North Africa and its natural connexion with Spain across the straits of Gibraltar.

In the fourth century, the vicars and most of the provincial governors had no military functions. From what we know of the command of the

---

[1] *C* 17896.   [2] Pallu de Lessert, *op. cit.* s.v. Numidia.
[3] Celsinus Titianus (380), Nicomachus Flavianus (377), Faltonius Probus Alypius (378).

1-2

armed forces in Africa, it seems clear that the separation of military from civil authority took place later there than elsewhere. During the second half of the third century, the provincial governors had had charge of the troops in their provinces, but when campaigns of any difficulty were undertaken it was usual for the armies to be concentrated under the command of an officer with the title of *dux*.[1] Clearly, this development was a step on the way to the complete separation of military from civil responsibility. In some provinces Diocletian took away control of the army from the provincial governors, but a recently discovered inscription shows this not to have been the case in Africa.[2]

Impp. DD. NN. Diocletiano et Maximiano aeternis Augg. et Constantio et Maximiano fortissimis Caesaribus principibus juventutis centenarium quod Aqua Viva appellatur ex praecepto Val. Alexandri v.p.agent.vic.praeff. praet. et Val.Flori v.p.p(raesidis) Numidiae a solo fabricatum curante Val.Ingenuo praep(osito) limit(is) dedicatum DD.NN.Diocletiano VIII et Maximiano VII Augg. conss. (A.D. 303.)

Thus the orders for the construction of the fort came to the commander of the *limes* through the governor of the province from the vicar of Africa. The first *comes Africae*—the style of the army commander after the separation was complete—must therefore be Constantinian, and in fact we know of none before Gratianus, the father of Valentinian, who held the position between 330 and 340. It is, however, probable that the change had taken place by about 316 when the *dux* Ursacius exercised the same powers as those of the later *comites*.[3] On the other hand, for a large part of the fourth century the *praesides* of Tripolitania[4] and Mauretania Caesariensis commanded troops, perhaps only on occasions, and probably only *limitanei*.[5] The power of the *comites* increased as the imperial government grew weaker, and towards the end of Roman rule in Africa they seem to be in complete control, and the provincial governors almost powerless. Mauretania Tingitana, though small in area, was of importance because of its position on the straits;

---

[1] E.g. *C* 12296. [2] *AE* (1942/3), 84.

[3] Pallu de Lessert, *op. cit.* s.v. Ursacius; see also above, p. 2, for the significance of the transfer of the Numidian capital from the military centre of Lambaesis to Cirta at about this time.

[4] *AE* (1948), 39 (c. 317), *C* 11031 (c. 355–60), *IRT* 565 (late fourth century) show governors of Tripolitania with military duties, but by 393, there was a *dux et corrector limitis Tripolitani* (*Cod. Theod.* XII. 1. 133); see also *Notit. Dig. Occ.* XXX. For Mauretania Caesariensis there is less evidence, and the *Notitia* is confused; we have a *praeses* (*Occ.* XIX) and a *dux limitis* (*Occ.* I. 38, V. 134) presumably separate; but also a *dux et praeses* (*Occ.* XXIX). [5] Below, p. 15, 16.

the troops there were commanded not by a governor with the additional title of *dux* as in Tripolitania, but by a *comes*. Little is known of the careers of most of the counts of Africa and Tingitana outside these commands. Their military efficiency was hardly tested throughout the century, and the obscurity in which they remain probably indicates that officers of only second-rate ability were sent there. Africa had, indeed, become a military backwater as early as the middle of the third century[1] and no new problem had arisen there in the intervening period.

The governors and counts were assisted by a staff of permanent civil servants. Though doubtless these were more numerous than they had been in the early imperial period, it may be noted that, where we have exact figures for their numbers, they are small considering the size of the area administered. The staff of the proconsul of Africa was supposed to number 400,[2] and that of the vicar of Africa only 300,[3] though the latter had five provinces subordinate to him. This may be explained by the fact that the vicar had little executive authority over his governors save in larger matters of policy and as a superior judge. We have no details for the staffs of the other governors, save from the Album of Thamugadi.[4] At that city in 362/3 were stationed thirty-seven officials subordinate to the governor of Numidia. Though not the capital, Thamugadi was the largest city of the province apart from Cirta, and was undoubtedly the centre of a considerable administrative district. The presence at Thamugadi of twenty-three officials belonging to the office of the *praefectus annonae*[5] confirms this; the produce from the fertile strip of land along the northern slopes of the Aures was evidently collected at Thamugadi for transmission through Cirta to the ports on the northern coast.

It would be wrong to minimize the corruption of the imperial civil service in this century; the evidence for its being widespread is too considerable to be ignored.[6] In general, the later the date the worse the position was. A law[7] of Constantine (in which there seems to be an authentic record of one of his outbursts of rage) begins:

Cessent iam nunc rapaces officialium manus, cessent, inquam; nam nisi moniti cessaverint, gladiis praecidentur.

---

[1] E. Birley, *JRS* xl (1950), 67–8.   [2] *Cod. Theod.* I. 12. 6 (398).

[3] *Cod. Theod.* I. 15. 5 (365).   [4] *C* 2403–17903.

[5] For this office, see below, p. 61.

[6] See Seeck, *Geschichte des Untergangs der antiken Welt*, II, 101–6.

[7] *Cod. Theod.* I. 16. 7 (331).

The rapacity of the officials which provoked this outburst consisted in the exaction of gratuities from litigants and others desirous of the speedy working of the official machine. Yet these gratuities were officially graded[1] according to the rank of the official by the governor of Numidia in 362/3. The violence of the language in the Code is not a clear measure of the immensity of the crimes forbidden. Other specific references to oppression in Africa of a worse type by the lower ranks of the service are scanty,[2] but the misdeeds of Romanus, the *comes Africae* between 363 and 373, were immortalized by Ammianus Marcellinus.[3] He refused to assist the province of Tripolitania when it was attacked unless they provided supplies. Even before him, the law forbidding requisition of food by the *comes Africae* had been broken.[4]

During this period also the term of office of the African governors—at least of the proconsuls—became very short; this allowed the permanent officials in the provinces to carry on their extortions with greater ease.

It was undoubtedly in an effort to deal with corruption by the governors and their officials that the institution of the *concilium provinciae* was encouraged by emperors of the fourth century.[5] That this was not a mere survival from the earlier Empire is shown by the fact that new provinces formed by Diocletian had *concilia*—for example Byzacena, Tripolitania and Mauretania Sitifensis. Thus the setting-up of these provincial councils was a deliberate act of policy. Their original purpose, the celebration of the imperial cult, naturally lost its significance under the Christian Empire. They continued, however, to be responsible for the administration of temple property and the celebration of provincial games; but, above all, they provided some slight outlet for the complaints of the provinces or for their feelings of loyalty. Even in the early Empire there had been cases of accusations made against governors by provincial councils.[6] During the fourth century, over half the laws under the title 'de legatis et decretis legationum'[7] deal with provincial assemblies. The most noteworthy example of their activity in Africa was the attempt in 364 by the provincial council of Tripolitania to complain to the emperor against

---

[1] C 17896.   [2] But see *Cod. Theod.* VIII. 10. 2.
[3] See below, p. 9.   [4] *Cod. Theod.* VII. 4. 3 (357).
[5] See Larsen, *Classical Philology*, XXIX (1934), 209 ff.
[6] E.g. Pliny, *Ep.* v. 20; C 11017.   [7] *Cod. Theod.* XII. 12.

Romanus.[1] Some legislation was actually addressed to the provincial councils.[2] As was to be expected, such an institution was not regarded with favour by the officials or the governors. The circumvention of the complaint of the Tripolitanians by high officials at the palace showed how justice could be prevented;[3] and the ineffectiveness of the councils is further shown by a law of 392 making the attendance of certain classes compulsory.[4] They were, in any case, representative only of a section of the wealthy provincials—the *primates*, or richest of the *curiales* (members of municipal councils), the *sacerdotales* (lawyers and *ex-curialibus*) and *honorati* (former high officials). Members of the senatorial order, normally the wealthiest and most powerful inhabitants, were not included; they could protect themselves.

[1] Amm. Marc. XXVIII. 6. 1–30.
[2] E.g. *Cod. Theod.* XII. 12. 9 (382), XII. 1. 59 (364).
[3] Amm. Marc. XXVIII. 6. 1–30.
[4] *Cod. Theod.* XII. 12. 12; compulsion was to be applied by the very persons who might be in danger from an accusation.

CHAPTER II

MILITARY HISTORY

AT the beginning of the reigns of Diocletian and Maximian, there were dangerous and widespread revolts in Africa. In 288, the Bavares, Quinquegentanei and other tribes rose, and the area of disturbance stretched from the Kabylie mountains in the north of Mauretania Sitifensis to the region of Tiaret. There was also trouble from tribes beyond the Saharan frontier to the south of the Hodna salt-marsh.[1] The revolt was suppressed by Aurelius Litua, a very active governor:[2] but the pacification was incomplete, and in 297 Maximian arrived in Africa in person. During the next eighteen months the emperor, with reinforcements from Gaul, traversed the whole of Africa from Mauretania Tingitana to Carthage.[3] It is possible that these risings were connected with the devastations of Frankish pirates in the Mediterranean[4] following the usurpation of Carausius in Britain and the consequent loss of the Roman fleet which controlled the Channel and North Sea. However that may be, this time the suppression of the Moors was complete. It was two generations before they again gave trouble. The emperors took this opportunity to make a thorough over-haul of the defences of Africa,[5] and widespread repairs were made to the system of roads.[6]

The area affected by the revolts of the Moors was limited to the wilder parts of Mauretania. The peace and security which the more settled provinces had long enjoyed were interrupted shortly after the abdication of Diocletian. Africa Proconsularis and part of Numidia suffered a repetition in a greater or lesser degree of the devastations which followed the suppression of an unsuccessful imperial claimant which she had suffered once before in the early third century. Maxentius,

---

[1] *C* 20215 (restoration of a fort destroyed by the Bavares); Jerome, *Chron. An.* 2304 (Quinquegentanei); *AE* (1912), 24 (fighting near Tiaret); *C* 9324 (fighting against 'barbari transtagnenses').

[2] He appears on the above inscriptions.

[3] *AE* (1939), 167 (Maximian at Tamuda in Tingitana; see also Seston, *op. cit.* 118); *AE* (1928), 39 (Maximian at Sitifis); *C* 8836 (at Tubusuctu); Elmer, *Zeitschrift für Numism.* xxv (1932), 22 ff.

[4] Seston, *op. cit.* 116 ff.   [5] See below, p. 23.

[6] C. van Sickle, *Class. Philol.* xxv (1930), 175 ff.

who was proclaimed Caesar at Rome in 306, was at once recognized in Africa; but when he broke with Maximian and Constantine in 308, the army in Africa, which had been devoted to the former since his victories over the Moors, withdrew its allegiance. Since Maximian was in no position to extend his own authority to Africa, the troops, after an attempt to get to Egypt, invested the vicar of Africa, Domitius Alexander, with the purple.[1] Alexander was certainly recognized throughout Africa Proconsularis and most of Numidia;[2] and if, as is unlikely, the troops in Mauretania did not join him, they made no effort to help Maxentius. Alexander must also have been supported by the wealthy classes in Africa. In 311 a small force sent by Maxentius dispersed the African army at the first shock. His revenge is thus described; 'Maxentius Carthaginem terrarum decus, simul Africae pulchriora vastari diripi incendique jusserat'. The chief city to suffer, apart from Carthage, was Cirta.[3] Another authority records the persecution of those remarkable for their birth or wealth.[4] After the defeat and death of Maxentius (312) Constantine went so far as to indulge the African population by sending his rival's head to Carthage.

No further important incidents in the political or military history of Africa occur till well into the second half of the century. The usurpation of Magnentius, who was recognized in Africa, does not seem to have had any adverse results. Ceionius Italicus was governor of Numidia before the death of Constans, remained under Magnentius, and was still governor a year after the recovery of Africa by Constantius.[5] Early in 361, when Constantius heard of the elevation of Julian by the army of Gaul, he sent a special commissioner to Africa to prevent it from falling to the new Augustus.[6] No hostilities took place.

In 363, however, occurred the first serious outbreak for half a century. This did not originate, as before, in the mountainous areas of Mauretania, but in the deserts to the south and east of Tripolitania. The tribe of the Austuriani invaded that province and devastated the fertile lands up to the walls of Lepcis Magna. Left unprotected owing to the inaction of Romanus, the *comes Africae*, who demanded the impossible subvention of 4000 camels and supplies as the price for his help, the

---

[1] Maurice, *Numismatique constantinienne*, I, 355–7.
[2] C 7004 (Cirta). [3] Aurelius Victor, *Caesares*, XL. 19 and 28.
[4] Zosimus II, 16. Maxentius was notorious for this sort of thing.
[5] C 7012; *Cod. Theod.* I. 15. 3. [6] Amm. Marc. XXI. 7. 2.

province was twice devastated again in the succeeding years, and Lepcis was besieged.[1] In the same year as this latter event it was feared that the usurper Procopius, who had raised a revolt in the East, might make an attempt on Africa and Valentinian took special measures for its defence.[2] No attack occurred, however. Militarily speaking, the Tripolitanian affair was of very small moment, and the only reason why Ammianus devoted such a considerable amount of space to it was presumably that the chief sufferers were a few individuals of the class of *curiales*, with which the historian was in sympathy. Though Romanus' actions, as recounted by Ammianus, cannot be judged as other than vicious, it ought to be considered that the pay of his troops was in arrears,[3] and that if a campaign into the desert against the Austuriani was to be undertaken, camels were a necessity.

Romanus, in spite of his conduct in leaving Tripolitania unprotected, continued to hold his command through the protection of powerful friends at court, who used every device to prevent the complaints of the province from being fairly heard. His rapacity was such that Ammianus Marcellinus used the example to illustrate his argument that Valentinian's greatest fault was allowing too much licence to the higher military officers.[4] While he was still in Africa, there occurred the most serious revolt for nearly a century,[5] involving the tribes who had been suppressed by Maximian in 297–8, and had since been quiet, though left in semi-independence in the mountains of Mauretania. According to Ammianus, a native chieftain, Firmus, killed one of his brothers, Zammac by name, a favourite of Romanus, and when prevented by the friends of the count from having his excuses presented to Valentinian, revolted. That there was more to it than this is clear. Many supported the grave charges (unspecified by Ammianus) which Romanus sent to Valentinian. The dispute was probably about the chieftainship— Firmus was a legitimate son of a former chief, Zammac the son of one of his concubines. Further, an inscription found in the Kabylie mountains, where the revolt began, indicates the site of a *praedium Sammacis*,[6] and declares its owner's loyalty to Rome. Ammianus refers to this estate, giving its owner's name as Salmaces, brother of Firmus.

---

[1] Amm. Marc. xxviii. 6. 4–13.   [2] Amm. Marc. xxvi. 5. 14.
[3] Amm. Marc. xxviii. 5. 12.   [4] Amm. Marc. xxvii. 9. 1–5.
[5] A detailed account is in Amm. Marc. xxix. 5. 2–56.
[6] Dessau, *ILS* 9351.

This name has presumably been incorrectly transmitted, for there can be little doubt that Sammac is identical with Firmus' victim. He probably relied on Romanus' support for some claim or other and made explicit his pro-Roman sympathies, while the extent and vigour of the revolt indicate that Firmus represented a certain amount of national feeling—or at least loyalty to a legitimate chief. The war was, perhaps, considered as the result of meddling by Romanus, for as soon as the *magister equitum* Theodosius arrived to take over the campaign, he arrested Romanus and his second-in-command, an action which somewhat vitiates Ammianus' account of the strength of Romanus' friends at court. Icosium and Caesarea were sacked, and Tipasa besieged. Theodosius (the father of the emperor) was summoned from Gaul with only a small force. Having joined the army in Africa he finally succeeded in crushing the revolt in a series of campaigns which lasted two years and extended over most of Mauretania Sitifensis and Caesariensis.[1]

A nationalist character is not so evident in the revolt of Gildo. This man was another brother of Firmus, and had assisted the Romans against him. It seems likely that he was appointed *comes Africae* by Maximus in 387 after the expulsion of Valentinian II from Italy.[2] Maximus himself had probably served with the elder Theodosius against Firmus;[3] and the first troops from the army in Gaul which supported his attempt were Moorish cavalry.[4] Gildo supplied Maximus with the African supplies over which he had control,[5] and when in 388 Theodosius decided to overthrow the usurper, he considered it necessary to make defensive dispositions on the Egyptian frontier with Africa.[6] Gildo escaped the fate of Maximus, and advanced in power. At some later date, his daughter was married to Nebridius, nephew of the Empress Flaccilla.[7] The ambitions of Gildo were again displayed between 392 and 394 during the usurpation of Eugenius at Rome. Though he did not openly break with Theodosius, Gildo continued to supply the capital with the African corn which was so essential to it, and refused to help the emperor in his campaign against Eugenius.[8]

---

[1] See below, p. 72, for the possibility of changes on the frontier consequent on this campaign.

[2] *Contra*, Seeck, *P-W* VII, 1360 puts the date of his appointment as *comes Africae* in 385, before Maximus obtained control of Italy.

[3] Amm. Marc. XXIX. 5. 6 and 21; Ensslin, *P-W* XIV, 2546.

[4] Ensslin, *ibid.* 2547.   [5] Pacatus, *Paneg.* 38. 2.

[6] Mitteis, *Papyr. Leipz.* I, 63.   [7] Jerome, *Ep.* 79.

[8] Symm. *Ep.* VI. 1; Claudian, *de Bell. Gild.* 246.

After the death of Theodosius in 395 his pretensions grew; he inter-
fered with the corn supply sufficiently to give cause for alarm about his
intentions, and finally, in 397, withdrew his allegiance from Honorius
and transferred it to Arcadius, emperor of the East. Though Gildo's
action was presumably designed to further his own ambitions, it was
welcomed at Constantinople and civil governors were sent to Africa by
Arcadius.[1] It is just as likely that Gildo wished to have a position like
that of Stilicho as that he meditated a completely independent Africa.
Orosius, writing in Africa with the possibility of talking with persons
involved,[2] gives not his own opinion, but those of two different sides,
the first that Gildo transferred his allegiance to Arcadius 'quadam
permotus invidia', the second that he withdrew Africa 'a societate
reipublicae...gentili magis licentia contentus quam ambitu regiae
affectationis inflatus'.[3] Early in 398, Honorius—or rather the all-
powerful Stilicho—sent yet another brother of Firmus with an inconsiderable force to recover the province. Gildo certainly received
support from the Moorish tribes, but when he met the imperial forces
near Theveste his army disintegrated almost without a blow being
struck.[4] Gildo, like his brother, supported the Donatist schismatics;
but having regard for the exemplary orthodoxy and piety of his female
relatives,[5] this is likely to have been from policy rather than conviction.
In the event, the Donatists gave him no more help than the Moors. The
appointment as *comes Africae*, in succession to Gildo, of Bathanarius,
brother-in-law of Stilicho who was supreme at the court of Honorius,
shows that the position was now held to be of first importance, doubtless because of the extreme dependence of Rome and Italy on food
imported from Africa. The relative security and prosperity of the area
also increased its desirability as a command for prominent soldiers.
Bathanarius remained in Africa till he was involved in the fall of
Stilicho. He was succeeded in 409 by Heraclian, who had killed the
great Vandal with his own hand and thus obtained the trust or gratitude
of Olympius, the new *magister officiorum*. Later in the same year Alaric
proclaimed Attalus as emperor at Rome. Heraclian refused to recognize

---

[1] Seranus, *procos. Afr.* late in 397. See Pallu de Lessert *op. cit.* III; inscriptions from
Thuburbo Maius (*AE* 1914, 57) and from Cirta (*C* 7017) dating between 395 and 402 have
the names of the proconsul and *consularis* respectively erased. They were probably
nominees of Arcadius, condemned after Gildo's fall.

[2] Orosius, VII. 36. 12.   [3] Orosius, VII. 36. 3.

[4] Orosius, VII. 36. 10.   [5] Jerome, *Ep.* 79.

this nominee of the Goths, and, remaining loyal to Honorius, cut off the food supply with the usual results.[1] After the defeat of an expedition sent by Attalus, Alaric himself attempted to cross into Africa in 410 after the sack of Rome, but his fleet was destroyed in a storm. Shortly afterwards Alaric died and the danger passed. Heraclian was now in a very powerful position and doubtless looked forward to enjoying the influence which Stilicho had exercised for so long. In fact, however, he was suspected of unspecified crimes and received no promotion,[2] although, so far as is known, he loyally supported the strong measures taken between 410 and 412 which finally crushed the Donatists. He revolted in the spring of 413, and instead of passively waiting for the imperial forces, embarked the army of Africa and landed in Italy. Orosius states that he had a fleet of some 3700 ships; this figure is clearly excessive, but the words of the historian[3] leave no doubt that Heraclian's force was formidable. It should be remembered that the whole of the fleet used to send corn to Rome was at his disposal. Heraclian advanced some distance, but was defeated at Otricoli[4] and after fleeing to Africa, was captured and executed late in 413.

If Firmus and, to a much lesser extent, Gildo represented the aspirations of the Moors, Heraclian was certainly supported in his opposition to Alaric and in his execution of the anti-Donatist measures by the Romanized upper class in the eastern part of Africa. During this time also numerous wealthy Romans took refuge in Africa. Jerome, who says that Heraclian acted harshly towards these refugees,[5] seems to be in error. Augustine and Orosius, better witnesses, have nothing bad to say about him, Orosius being restrained about the revolt, in contrast to his attitude towards other usurpers against the authority of Christian emperors.[6] Proba and Melania, two of the wealthiest refugees, found it better to live in Africa than to return to the devastated Western provinces.[7]

We now come to the final stages of the rule of Rome in Africa. About 423, Boniface, a soldier of some ability, was made *comes Africae*. Holding the province for the Empress Placidia and her young son Valentinian III, he defeated an attempt by the usurper Johannes to get control (424/5).[8] Despite this, Boniface was suspected of infidelity,

---

[1] Zosim. VI. 9.   [2] Orosius, VII. 42. 4–12.
[3] Orosius, *ibid.* 'immensa certe temporibus nostris satis incredibilis classis'.
[4] Hydat. *Continuatio chron. Hier.* 56 (*MGH* XI, 18).
[5] Jerome, *Ep.* 130.   [6] Orosius, VII. 42.   [7] Aug. *Ep.* 150, written in 414.
[8] Prosper Tiro, *Epit. chron.* 1286 (*MGH* IX, 420).

especially when he married an Arian. In 427 he rejected a summons to return to the court, and defeated an expedition sent by Placidia to recover Africa.[1] At the same time some tribes rose and caused great devastations.[2] In the following year another expedition was sent from Rome under the German Sigisvult with an army of Goths. Boniface did not, apparently, oppose him, but retired to Sitifis.[3] Owing to the influence of Augustine and others, Boniface was reconciled to Placidia, and Sigisvult was withdrawn.[4] Meanwhile, however, Boniface had invited the Vandals into Africa to help him against Sigisvult.[5] In seeking barbarian aid, he was, of course, merely doing what most important generals from Stilicho to Aetius had done. Geiseric, the king of the Vandals, was delayed by a revolt in Spain, but crossed into Africa early in 429 with his whole race. Boniface, restored to favour, now sought to oppose the Vandals, who demonstrated at once that they were bent on conquest and permanent settlement.[6] He was heavily defeated somewhere in Mauretania, and retreated to Hippo Regius.[7] This town was invested in 430, but was still holding out in the summer of 431. Reinforcements arrived from Constantinople, but a second defeat of the imperial forces near Calama was final. The Vandals quickly overran the rest of Africa, only a few walled cities holding out. Carthage was captured in 439.

Study of the Roman military forces in Africa[8] from the end of the third century is difficult because of the almost complete lack of epigraphical evidence and the controversial nature of the literary sources. The African army was, like that of all the other provinces, entirely reorganized by Diocletian and Constantine. It had formerly consisted of one legion, the III Augusta, with its auxiliaries. When reorganized at the end of the third century, it was divided into a field army and a static frontier force. The establishment of the former in North Africa under the command of the *comes Africae* was as follows:

Infantry	3 *legiones palatinae* of 1000 men	3,000
	8 *legiones comitatenses* of 1000	8,000
	1 *auxilium palatinum* of 500 men	500
Cavalry	19 *vexillationes comitatenses* of 500 men	9,500
	Total strength	21,000

[1] *MGH* IX, 421. [2] Aug. *Ep.* 220. 7. [3] Aug. *Ep.* 229.
[4] Aug. *Ep.* 230. [5] Procopius, *de Bell. Vand.* I. 3. [6] Victor de Vita, I. 1.
[7] Procopius, *de Bell. Vand.* I. 3. 31.
[8] Cagnat, *L'Armée romaine d'Afrique* is an essential work.

The names of all these formations are given in the *Notitia Dignitatum*.[1] The numerical strength of this force is estimated to have been slightly above that which had sufficed in the early Empire.[2] It need hardly be said that the legions of Diocletian had little but the name in common with those of an earlier period. The most noteworthy point is that the nineteen squadrons of cavalry represented the strongest force of its kind in the Empire.

This force was the regular army of the North African provinces. It is to be regarded as a mobile or reserve force not because it was necessarily stationed in the interior of the provinces but to distinguish it from the force of peasant-soldiers who carried out the defence of the actual frontier. These men, the *limitanei*, held their land on condition that they defended the frontier region in which they lived when called upon. Although organized in a semi-military fashion the *limitanei* were essentially peasants and did not receive pay. Owing to their importance in the social history of North Africa, a separate chapter is devoted to the frontier system and its defenders.[3]

Certain obscurities in the sections of the *Notitia Dignitatum* dealing with Africa must now be discussed, particularly as important conclusions about the military history of North Africa at the end of the fourth century have been drawn from them. While the *comes Africae* is shown as having a large regular force under his command,[4] the *duces* of Tripolitania and Mauretania Caesariensis control *limitanei* only.[5] There has never been any suggestion that the section of the *Notitia* which lists the regular forces of the Empire is incomplete, and it would be wrong to postulate an omission. It may well be, as has been suggested,[6] that Tripolitania was considered too small a stretch of territory to have regular forces stationed in it—though this can hardly have been the case between 355 and 361 when an incursion of barbarians was defeated by the governor Fl. Archontius Nilus.[7] The same cannot be said of Mauretania. As has been shown above, important revolts during the third and fourth centuries took place in that area, which was in fact militarily the most dangerous in Africa. It thus seems likely that by the time the *Notitia* was written, all the regular forces in Africa were

---

[1] *Occ.* VII.
[2] Cagnat, *L'Armée romaine d'Afrique*, 731. The figures for each unit must be regarded as very approximate.
[3] Below, Ch. III.   [4] *Occ.* VII.   [5] *Occ.* XXX and XXXI.
[6] Cagnat, *op. cit.* 734.   [7] *C* 11031.

concentrated in the hands of the *comes Africae*. We have another indication of the encroachment of this officer on the *dux Mauretaniae* in the list of *limes* sectors. Three of these are noted as being under the command of both *comes* and *dux*.[1] It is also significant that in the detailed accounts of the incursions of the Austuriani into Tripolitania (363–5) and the revolt of Firmus in Mauretania (372–4), Ammianus Marcellinus mentions neither *duces* nor provincial governors as having any important part in the military operations. The separation of powers is particularly noticeable in the former instance. No mention is made of any initial action taken by Ruricius, the governor; it was the city council of Lepcis which requested help from the *comes Africae*. When Romanus had come and gone with his forces, a further request, granted only to be withdrawn almost at once, was that the command of military operations should be added to the civil duties of the governor.[2] The *duces* or governors of these provinces, therefore, controlled only the *limitanei*;[3] any operation requiring larger forces was the responsibility of the *comes Africae*. It was through their command of all the troops in Africa that the *comites* Romanus, Gildo and Heraclian attained their power.

Deserving of consideration is the question why in the section[4] of the *Notitia* entitled 'Distributio numerorum' the *comes Africae* and *comes Tingitanae* are shown as commanding considerable forces, while in the sections devoted to the details of their commands no troops other than *limitanei*[5] are included. It has been suggested by F. Lot[6] that the former sections represent the order of battle in Africa in the middle of the fourth century, and that after the revolt of Firmus, or at latest after the revolt of Gildo, all regular forces were withdrawn from Africa, which had henceforth to depend for its defence solely on *limitanei*. Thus the chapters giving *limitanei* only to the *comites* of Africa and Mauretania Tingitana would be of late date, probably early fifth century. There is, however, much evidence that considerable forces remained in Africa long after the revolt of Firmus.

In the first place, among the cavalry units mentioned in the 'Distri-

---

[1] *Occ.* XXV and XXX; the *limites* of Columnata, Caputcellae, and Bida.

[2] Amm. Marc. XXVIII. 6. 11; 'negotiorum quoque militarium cura praesidi delata'.

[3] *Cod. Theod.* VII. 15. 1 (409), containing provisions about the property and duties of *limitanei*, is addressed to the vicar of Africa, the superior of the civil governors.

[4] *Occ.* VII.   [5] *Occ.* XXV and XXVI.

[6] Lot, *Revue des études anciennes*, XXXVIII (1936), 309–10.

butio numerorum' as being under the command of the *comes Africae* occur the 'Equites Honoriani Juniores';[1] this unit took its name from Honorius who became emperor in 395. There also appear the 'Equites Marcomanni'[2] who must have been organized after the entry of that tribe into the Empire in 396 or 397 and could hardly have been in Africa till after the suppression of Gildo in 398.

It is argued that to defeat the revolts of Firmus and Gildo, Gaul was emptied of its best elements.[3] If this were true it would show that the African army was already too small to deal effectively with Firmus' Moorish tribes: on the other hand, at least two, probably four, units mentioned by Ammianus in his narrative of Firmus' revolt are in the *Notitia*. The *pedites Constantiani* can hardly be other than the *Constantiaci* of the *Notitia*;[4] the *equites quartae sagittariorum cohortis* are in the *Notitia* as 'Equites quarto sagittarii'.[5] In the reference to the 'primam et secundam legionem' stationed by Theodosius at Caesarea we may see the Leg. I Fl. Pacis and Leg. II Fl. Virtutis.[6] Gildo is said to have mustered a force of 70,000 men.[7] Although this figure is certainly exaggerated, Gildo could never have thought of revolt if he had had no regular troops under his command, especially as his strength among the Moors was small compared with that which Firmus had had. Thus Lot's argument would indicate that the regular army he commanded was considerable. In fact, however, the troops brought from Europe to Africa on these occasions were by no means numerous, though in the case of the campaign against Gildo they were probably of good quality.[8] It may further be noted that the title of 'magister utriusque militiae' conferred upon Gildo about 393, while doubtless honorific, would have been meaningless unless he had been in command of an army of some size.[9]

When we turn to the attempt of Heraclian, the presence of a regular army is again manifest. He did not wait for a punitive expedition to sail for Africa, but made an attempt on Italy himself. If we may judge

---

[1] *Occ.* VII. 196.   [2] *Occ.* VII. 183.

[3] Lot, *loc. cit.*   [4] Amm. Marc. XXIX. 5. 20; *Notit. Occ.* V. 252.

[5] Amm. Marc. *ibid.*; *Notit. Occ.* VII.

[6] Amm. Marc. XXIX. 5. 18; *Notit. Occ.* V. 250, 251.

[7] Orosius, VII. 36. 6.

[8] Claudian, *de Bell. Gild.* V. 420 ff. See Cagnat, *op. cit.* 733.

[9] *Cod. Theod.* IX. 7. 91. The title was just coming into use, and was held by such powerful generals as Ricimer (*Cod. Theod.* VII. 1. 13, 381) and Stilicho (*Cod. Theod.* VII. 5. 1, 399).

from the numbers—doubtless exaggerated, but representing something considerable—of ships used and the casualties at the battle of Otricoli where Heraclian was defeated, his forces were large.[1] It might be held that this disaster was the end of the African army. However, Augustine, writing to Count Boniface about 427, contrasts the latter's vigour when he defeated Moorish raids (probably between 414 and 422) as tribune of a few *foederati* (barbarian mercenaries) with his later inactivity as *comes Africae* despite 'tam magnus exercitus et potestas' under his command.[2] The contrast is obvious. Boniface was further able to defeat two attempts on Africa from Italy and meet the Vandals in a final if unsuccessful battle. By this time, the African army probably had a larger German element. In addition to the *equites Marcomanni* mentioned in the *Notitia*, the *foederati* who sustained the siege of Hippo Regius with Boniface in 430 were Goths.[3]

It is, of course, just possible that for a short period Africa was without regular troops, but there is not a single piece of evidence to support this hypothesis, and consequently no information as to when a withdrawal could have taken place. It seems far more likely that a considerable force remained in Africa to the end. This, after all, is only natural when we consider the importance of Africa as a source of food for Rome and Italy. Such a province was not to be left to the care of *limitanei* alone, especially after 410 when it was the only part of the West undevastated by the Germans. We have no evidence to establish whether or not there were regular forces in Mauretania Tingitana at a later date; but since the province was strategically and administratively part of Spain, its retention was essential if control of the straits of Gibraltar was to be maintained. Only when the Goths and Vandals arrived in Spain is it likely that troops were taken from Tingitana. It seems unwise, therefore, to try and draw conclusions as to the strength of the African army at a given date from anomalies in the *Notitia*.

In estimating the success of the Roman army in its defence of Africa, it must be admitted that the problems with which it was faced were by no means of the most difficult nature. It is clear that the Saharan deserts could not support a population large enough to prove a serious threat from outside, at least till the use of the camel had become widespread;[4]

---

[1] Orosius, VII. 42; see above, p. 13.   [2] Aug. *Ep.* 220. 7.
[3] Possidius, *Vita Augustini*, 28.
[4] Gautier, *Les Siècles obscures du Mahgreb, passim.*

and further that the mountainous areas inside the frontier, though only partially subdued, were likewise thinly populated.[1] For these reasons, the replacement of the Romans by the Vandals brought no change on the frontiers or in dangerous parts of the interior of the provinces for some time; there were no revolts in the mountains till between 480–90, and the invasions from the desert which began about 523 were the first of a series lasting over two centuries in which the nomads completely destroyed civilization in North Africa. The chief problem consisted, therefore, in dealing with raids by small bands rather than invasion on a large scale. The Austuriani, who raided Tripolitania in the years 363–5, are described by Ammianus[2] as 'in discursus semper expediti veloces, vivereque assueti rapinis et caedibus'; such was presumably the way of life of all the desert tribes. The cavalry force, the most useful arm against such raids, was the strongest of its kind in the Empire, and amounted to nearly half the strength of the African army. Compared with the struggles on the Rhine, Danube and Euphrates the African wars were merely of a 'colonial' nature. For most of the fourth century, officers of only second-rate ability commanded there. Nevertheless the protection of the enormous area of North Africa by such a modest garrison was undoubtedly a considerable achievement. In keeping these provinces the securest in the Empire, the regular troops were assisted by a force of frontier guards, the *limitanei*, whose position must now be discussed.

[1] Sherwin-White, 'Geographical factors in Roman Algeria,' *JRS* xxiv (1944), 6 ff.
[2] Amm. Marc. xxviii. 6. 2.

CHAPTER III

THE FRONTIER AND ITS DEFENDERS

TOWARDS the end of the first century A.D., when the expansion of the Roman Empire had almost ceased, a system of permanent defences along its frontiers was begun. The word used for such a system—*limes*—denoted not only some material barrier designed to exclude the barbarians from the Empire, whether natural, like the Rhine on the boundary of Gaul, or artificial like Hadrian's Wall in Britain, but the forts, camps, and road communications behind the frontier line and the outposts and signal towers thrown out in advance of it. The *limes* was in fact a system of defence in depth; the outposts and the natural or artificial barrier, besides being necessary for the strict control of movement on the frontiers, could also delay attackers until reserves from the camps behind the line could be concentrated. The barrier, if substantial enough, protected the provinces from any but well-organized and numerous bands and thus freed them from the danger of frequent small but destructive raids.

The long southern frontier of Africa presented a difficult problem as natural barriers were almost entirely lacking, though the position was not as bad as it might have been owing to the relatively small population outside the frontier. The Sirtic desert, the Hammadra el-Hamra plateau and the Grand Erg Oriental were certainly obstacles to potential invaders of the coastal plain of Tripolitania, and the Chott Djerid gave similar protection to the south of Byzacena: but such deserts were not completely impassable, and were not continuous. Along the whole of the southern flank of the Aures range, there was no natural defence line. North-west of Gemellae, the salt-marsh of the Hodna provided a substantial barrier against incursion into Mauretania Sitifensis, but, west of that again, the limit of Roman power was a practically featureless area of steppe country until the river Chelif was reached. To the south and west of that river, the very extent and chronology of Roman occupation are obscure, though it is possible that in the early Empire at least a frontier road between Mauretania Caesariensis and Mauretania

Tingitana ran through the pass known as Trik-es-Soltan.[1] The southern boundary of Tingitana, running just south of Fez in the second and third centuries, was withdrawn to a small area enclosing the peninsula of Tangier during the reign of Diocletian.

Artificial barriers were thus required to make up for the lack of natural defences. That these existed was known even before archaeological confirmation was obtained, because a law of later date refers to a *limes* and *fossatum* in Africa.[2] *Limes*, as usual, means the whole defensive system of the frontier, while the *fossatum* is an artificial barrier consisting of a ditch and wall. Only slight traces of the *fossatum* were known until recently. These were on the frontier of Mauretania Tingitana near Fez and to the south-west of the Aures covering the region of Gemellae.[3] Air photography has recently revealed three more sections of considerable length.[4] The first, like the latter of those mentioned above, is to the south of the Aures, but about a hundred miles due east of Gemellae. It runs along the Dj. Majour near the fort of Ad Majores and bars the routes from the desert into southern Byzacena between the Aures and the Chott Djerid. A second discovery was of a stretch of *fossatum* to the west of the Aures and north of Gemellae. Here, the fortification runs in a north-westerly direction from Mesarfelta to Thubunae, cutting diagonally the main routes from the south-west into Numidia.

The location of the third newly discovered stretch of *fossatum* gives a further indication of the difficulties the Romans had to face in their defence of Africa. It is not on the Saharan frontier at all, but cuts off the mountainous area of the Bou Taleb to the north of the Hodna from the fertile plains stretching north to Sitifis and east as far as Lambaesis and Thamugadi. The Bou Taleb was one of the several mountainous regions in the interior of Roman Africa which were only half subdued and which were for all practical purposes reserves for the Moorish tribes, and in which several dangerous revolts had their origin. The Bou Taleb is the only one which is so far proved to have been partly enclosed by a *fossatum*, but it is quite possible that the others were similarly defended, at least in places. There is some evidence for this in

---

[1] Carcopino, *Le Maroc antique*, 237 ff; but see E. W. Gray, *JRS* XXXVIII (1948), 122.
[2] *Cod. Theod.* VII. 15. 1 (409).
[3] Carcopino, *op. cit.* 233 ff., and Gsell, *Mélanges Boissier*, 227 ff.
[4] J. Baradez, *Fossatum Africae*, part II.

the *Notitia Dignitatum*. In Africa, the defensive system was so extensive that in the fourth century it was divided into sectors, each of which was also called *limes* with the name of the sector headquarters to define it, and was under the command of a *praepositus*. The names of the sectors as they were constituted towards the end of Roman rule are given in the *Notitia*.[1] The Bou Taleb range was guarded not only by the *fossatum* but by a *limes* with its headquarters at Thamalluma; there was also a sector to the south, at Zabi, which would prevent the tribes from the desert joining with those of the mountains. Along the north coast of Africa, from the Oued El Kebir (the boundary between Numidia and Mauretania Sitifensis) in the east to Icosium in the west the lesser and greater Kabylie mountains were inhabited by the Bavares and Quinquegentanei who both gave considerable trouble. They were separated by the *limes* of Tubusuctu and supervised by the *limes Tuccensis* and the *limes Bidensis*. The Aures range, however, was not guarded. It seems to have been entirely peaceful in the third and fourth centuries;[2] to the north of the range, one of the most prosperous parts of Africa flourished in complete security, and the *limites* to the south and west of it faced the desert, not the mountains. Of these, the most easterly was Turris Tamalleni, on the boundary between Byzacena and Tripolitania; to the west of this, in the narrow stretch of fertile land between the mountains and the desert, there were sector headquarters at Nepta, Badias and Gemellae. To the west of the mountains the route into Numidia was protected by Thubunae.

The *limes* naturally extended along the southern frontier of Mauretania Caesariensis. Unfortunately, the place names west of Columnata cannot be identified with certainty.[3] The *limes* of Tripolitania, like that of Mauretania Caesariensis, was under the command of the *dux* of the province,[4] not the *comes Africae*. There, too, we cannot identify many of the sectors: from the number given in the *Notitia*[5] and the smallness of the province, we may deduce that they were not so extensive as in the rest of Africa.

[1] *Occ.* xxv, xxx, xxxi.

[2] Sherwin-White, *loc. cit.* 5, says that 'as a whole the Berber population of the Aures remained undisturbed and hostile'. This may have been so in the second century—the area was only encircled and penetrated by Trajan—but while it probably remained empty of Roman settlement, there is no evidence of disorder in the later period, a marked contrast to the Kabylie ranges.

[3] E.g. *limes inferior, limes Balaretani*.   [4] *Notit. Occ.* xxx, xxxi.

[5] *Ibid.* xxxi; twelve sectors, of which only three have been identified.

The date of the establishment of the *limes* in Africa is at present somewhat doubtful. Certainly, the area to be defended was so large that the work could hardly have been done in a single generation and what evidence we have shows variation from place to place. By analogy with other western provinces, a start should have been made about the beginning of the second century. At that time the frontier of Africa had only just been fixed. For instance, it was not till the reign of Trajan that a road was constructed along the south of the Aures. Clearly, from that time onwards some sort of defence against desert tribes was a necessity, and the Numidian *fossata* have been tentatively dated to Hadrian's reign.[1] In Tripolitania, however, it appears likely that the abandonment of a policy of controlling the tribes by punitive expeditions took place under Septimius Severus.[2] There is further evidence that the whole of the African *limes* was thoroughly reorganized during the reigns of Diocletian and Constantine, and perhaps it then reached its final form. Five of the six known *centenaria*[3]—the name given to small forts in the *limes*—are from this period, and located in widely separated areas.[4] It seems probable also that the office of *praepositus limitis* was introduced in the reign of Diocletian, but that at the time the frontier system was organized on a provincial basis.[5] Probably, when the command of the army was finally separated from the civil authority, the division of the *limes* into sectors as found in the *Notitia* took place. As a final indication of date, the fourth century was the most extensive period of activity in the Tripolitanian *limes*.[6]

The *limes* and *fossatum* have an important place in the social and economic life of Africa. By the time of Alexander Severus the task of defending the permanent frontiers had apparently become too large for the regular forces of the Empire. Where possible it began to be entrusted to *limitanei*.[7] These were men who were given land on the

---

[1] Baradez, *op. cit.* 161.

[2] R. G. Goodchild and J. B. Ward-Perkins, *JRS* xxxix (1949), 82.

[3] Derived from *centenarius*, the equivalent of *centurio* in the legions.

[4] *C* 22763 (Tibubuci, in Tripolitania, from the reign of Diocletian); *C* 20215 (repair of Aqua Frigida in the Lesser Kabylie, 293); *AE* (1942/3), 84 (Aqua Viva, between Gemellae and the Hodna, 303); *C* 8701 (Centenarium Solis, near Sitifis, 315); *C* 9010 (Bou Atelli, in the Djurjura Mts., 328). The other *centenarium* known is that of Gasr Duib, in Tripolitania, dated to 244–6 (Goodchild and Ward-Perkins, *loc. cit.* 91).

[5] *AE* (1942/3), 84, records a *praepositus limitis* with no territorial qualification under the orders of the *praeses Numidiae*. See also *C* 9025 for a *limes* (*Mauretaniae*).

[6] R. G. Goodchild, *BRS* xix (1951), 65.   [7] SHA, *Vita Alex. Sev.* 58.

frontiers on condition that they defended it when called upon. At first the *limitanei* were probably veterans; but their sons could inherit the land if they fulfilled the required military obligations. At some stage members of barbarian tribes were attracted from outside into these areas on the same conditions,[1] the land being entirely free from any other burden. The *limitanei* were organized in semi-military fashion; they were settled round *centenaria*.

The settlement of *limitanei* in Tripolitania is particularly well known.[2] In the east of that province, there is evidence of 'an area of *limitanei* settlements which in their extent, uniformity of pattern and degree of preservation are perhaps unique in the Roman world'.[3] Here have been found numerous fortified buildings indistinguishable from the official *centenaria* of the province. The number of associated mausolea and agricultural installations, particularly those to do with water supply, indicates, according to the archaeologists, not merely a series of outposts, but a widespread structure of society. None of the inscriptions relating to these buildings is earlier than the third century; many are certainly from the fourth.[4] If the earlier buildings were put up by legionaries or veterans, the later were probably built by natives; there are two Libyan inscriptions in which the word *centenarium* can be distinguished.[5]

Such a phenomenon has yet to be discovered in the other parts of Africa.[6] There is, however, the clearest indication that the *fossatum* marked not only a line of defence, but an economic frontier. Where it exists, it generally marks with great accuracy the division between cultivated land and the desert.[7] This is particularly noticeable to the south and west of the Aures. Rainfall in the mountain ranges is often considerable. The water if left to itself rushes with considerable violence down the mountains before losing itself in the desert.[8] The task of the *limitanei* was the same as that of the colonists along the north of the Aures, such as those of Thamugadi, namely to utilize these sudden

[1] *Cod. Theod.* VII. 15. 1. Though of late date (409), this law refers to much earlier practice.
[2] R. G. Goodchild and J. B. Ward-Perkins, 'The *Limes Tripolitanus*. I', *JRS* XXXIX (1949); R. G. Goodchild, 'The *Limes Tripolitanus*. II', *JRS* XL (1950); 'Roman sites on the Tarhuna plateau of Tripolitania', *BRS* XIX (1951).
[3] Goodchild and Ward-Perkins, *loc. cit.* 93.
[4] E.g. those associated with the mausolea at Ghirza, *C* 22660, 22661.
[5] Goodchild and Ward-Perkins, *loc. cit.* 94.
[6] It may be noted that no trace of *fossatum* has yet been found in Tripolitania. Did the density of *limitanei* settlement make it unnecessary?
[7] Baradez, *op. cit.* 171–215.   [8] *Ibid.* 171–84.

flows and prevent the destruction they caused through erosion. The efficiency and complexity of the installations created for this purpose in other parts of Africa are one of the best known features of Roman civilization in North Africa, and have been the subject of special studies.[1] The area where such works have been most frequently discovered is the northern slope of the Aures and Bou Taleb mountains where settlements were very numerous and, in the latter region, corn was grown on a large scale as it is today. In these areas there had been considerable settlement from the first century A.D. onwards. The fertility of the *limes* regions, on the other hand, may be ascribed almost entirely to the work of legionaries, veterans, and *limitanei*. Only in a few cases can signs of cultivation be found on the desert side of the *fossatum*. When we consider the thin strip of territory which divided the Aures mountains from the desert to the south, the consistent peacefulness of the inhabitants of the interior becomes still more manifest. The *limitanei* had to defend themselves only against the nomads of the desert, and had no fear for what might happen behind their backs.

The difference between the *limites* to the south and west of the Aures which faced the desert and those cutting off the Bou Taleb and Kabylie mountains from the fertile plains has been noted. Yet in the Bou Taleb area also, the *fossatum* marks the boundary between the cultivated area and the barren—only in this case the latter is not desert but forest.

The degree of romanization of the *limitanei* can only have been slight. When they were first organized in the reign of Alexander Severus, some were probably veterans from among the troops already garrisoning the frontier. But at this date most of the legionary troops were themselves of local origin, and there were also important Syrian elements among the auxiliaries. Later, land was given to barbarian tribes on the same conditions—as the law[2] puts it, 'propter curam munitionemque limitis atque fossati'. At Ghirza, in the *limes* of Tripolitania, there are inscriptions dating from the fourth century which record only Moorish names.[3] Doubtless even the barbarians who were given land in the *limites* adopted an entirely sedentary way of life and gradually became to that extent influenced by Rome through discipline and the co-operative effort needed to maintain the system.

---

[1] E.g. Du Coudray de la Blanchère, *Aménagement de l'eau dans l'Afrique ancienne*, comparing it with the present state of Tunisia.

[2] *Cod. Theod.* VII. 15. 1. 　　　　　　[3] *C* 22660, 22661.

That they became in some cases men of some wealth is shown by the ruins of the considerable mausolea of Ghirza.[1] The archaeology of this area also indicates an incipient feudalism,[2] with the *centenarii*—perhaps originally petty chieftains—gradually reducing their *limitanei* to a position of personal subjection. Yet it does not seem justifiable to suppose that the *limitanei* of Tripolitania were guilty of treachery and joined with the nomad Austuriani in their devastations of 363–5.[3] The whole point of the *limes* system in Africa was the establishment and the self-protection of settled farmers. Archaeological evidence seems to prove that the *limitanei* in Tripolitania were Christian, numerous and prosperous in the fourth century—and later.[4] However unmixed the racial origin of these, once firmly settled in Roman territory they had much to lose from an association with the tribes of the desert. It is explicitly stated that the nomadic Austuriani deliberately cut down the olive trees and vines in much of Tripolitania, and massacred the rural population.[5]

In the frontier regions of Numidia there can be little doubt that the defenders were somewhat more romanized. Behind them was, in most cases, a region of much more intensive Roman settlement. Further, some of the forts behind and in advance of the *fossatum* were garrisoned in the fourth century by regular soldiers.[6] It has already been noted that no serious breach in the desert frontier of Africa was made until the later part of the Vandal occupation.[7] During that period also the Moors and Romans of the western part of the Aures, including a part of the *limes*, formed an independent kingdom and fought against nomads from beyond the Hodna as well as mountaineers from the centre of the Aures.[8] Finally, the fertility due to the maintenance of irrigation was a source of admiration to the Arabs some two centuries later.[9] There can be little doubt that it was the self-sufficiency of the *limes* which enabled it to survive for so long the weakness and then the disappearance of Roman rule.

[1] Mathuisieulx, *Nouv. Arch. des Miss. Sc.* XII (1904), 22 ff.

[2] Goodchild and Ward-Perkins, *loc. cit.* 95.

[3] Amm. Marc. XXVIII. 6. 1–30. But see Goodchild and Ward-Perkins, *loc. cit.* 95, who suggest that the *limitanei* were guilty of neglect or treachery.

[4] R. G. Goodchild, *BRS* XIX (1951), 65.   [5] Amm. Marc. XXVIII. 6. 13.

[6] *Cod. Theod.* XI. 1. 11 (365) refers to the transport of the *annona* to the *limes Africae*. This would supply regular forces, not *limitanei* who had their own land.

[7] Procopius, III. 9. 3 records a dangerous Moorish attack on Byzacena *c.* 523.

[8] See below, pp. 74 ff.

[9] References in Gsell, *Atlas archéologique de l'Algérie*, s.v. Badias.

CHAPTER IV

THE CITIES

OUR knowledge of the fluctuations in the prosperity of the cities and towns of North Africa depends to a very large extent on epigraphical evidence, and perhaps even more so in the fourth century than in earlier periods. It hardly needs stating that such evidence can be misleading and has to be used with care. In North Africa, however, the inscriptions can legitimately be used both individually and in groups to amplify the scanty written accounts. The reason is that in contrast to the northern parts of the Empire where there were a few cities of considerable size and little else but villages and semi-tribal agglomerations, the characteristic of urban life in Africa was the large number of small towns with all the apparatus of the Roman municipal idea. This characteristic obtained not only in the proconsular province but in parts of Byzacena and Numidia as well. Many of the sites of the old towns have been more or less desolate since the end of Roman rule, and no events during that rule brought wide enough destruction to cause significant gaps in the epigraphy. So, while detailed archaeological studies of the sites are few, inscriptions have been noted on such a considerable scale in every part of the area where urban life predominated that it may be assumed that in general the known inscriptions of any period and district form a proper ratio to those which originally existed. The one important exception to this is Tripolitania, relevant inscriptions from which have almost all been found in the principal city, Lepcis Magna. This is owing to the exceptional amount of archaeological work carried out on a site in an excellent state of preservation. Tripolitanian inscriptions are, therefore, not used in the main argument which follows.

The period when the African cities were most flourishing began with the reign of Trajan and continued until that of Septimius Severus.[1] As the century progressed, the number of honorific dedications, public buildings and records of generosity by private citizens steadily increased. Many towns advanced in status or were formed from romanized

---

[1] See especially Sherwin-White, *Roman Citizenship*, 196, 197.

elements among the Numidian tribes. The increase in public buildings and dedications indicates not only that the towns were growing more prosperous all the time; it also shows that men of modest means had come to feel the desirability of leaving behind some memorial which should indicate their public spirit. The picture of urban life in Africa at this time, particularly in the reign of Septimius Severus, who, as an African, naturally evoked enthusiasm, is undeniably bright.

The decline in such exhibitions of public spirit after the death of Alexander Severus was sudden and complete. It is true that, as has been pointed out by Rostovtzeff,[1] Africa and Syria were little affected by the disasters which occurred in other provinces under the Severan dynasty. Africa in particular escaped the devastations of the civil wars and the relentless measures taken by Septimius against those areas from which his opponents had drawn support. His African origin must also have had a mitigating effect. But there as elsewhere his oppressive policy towards the upper classes of the city population bore heavily. The personal responsibility of magistrates for taxes and the system of liturgies were both developed by Septimius' jurists into permanent exactions,[2] enforced by the state. It is possible that the effects of this policy were not so marked in Africa, where urbanization was in large measure new and expanding, as in some of the eastern provinces where it had long been static or declining. Unfortunately it was at this moment that Africa, which had long escaped injury from war, became the scene of an imperial contest. In 238, the landowners from the region Thysdrus in the proconsular province revolted as a result of the fiscal exactions of Maximinus Thrax. They persuaded the elderly proconsul Gordian to assume the purple; but against the regular troops of the legate of Numidia, Capellianus, who remained faithful to Maximinus, Gordian was helpless. Capellianus executed the aristocracy of Carthage, and confiscated private fortunes and the money belonging to the city and the temples. He killed the prominent men in the other cities which had supported Gordian, and allowed his soldiers to pillage the countryside and the villages.[3] It does not appear that there was widespread destruction of the towns themselves; the silence of Herodian on this point is not disproved by archaeological evidence, and the short phrase to the contrary employed by the author of the life of Maximinus looks

---

[1] Rostovtzeff, *Social and Economic History of the Roman Empire*, 358, 600.
[2] See the title 'de muneribus et honoribus', *Dig.* 50. 4.   [3] Herodian, VII. 9–11.

conventional.[1] Nevertheless, the episode was a disaster because in view of the disturbed state of affairs in general and the increasing pressure on the upper classes in the towns, those of the wealthy who survived were naturally disposed to dissemble their wealth as much as possible, and because it was a manifestation of the hostility which appeared at times between some elements in the army and the romanized population of the cities. One of the few explicit references to this development is from a memorial to a victim of Capellianus.[2] In the fifty years separating the death of Gordian III (244) from the accession of Diocletian (284) only some half a dozen inscriptions have been found recording public building and benefactions. Expressions of loyalty to the emperors by the town councils or magistrates are likewise less numerous, especially in the southern part of the province (later called Byzacena), where the revolt originated; there appear to be no inscriptions recording any building or dedication to an emperor between 244 and 270; it is possible, therefore, that this part of Africa was the most injured by Capellianus.

This decline in public spirit and expenditure was paralleled all over the Empire and was a natural result of the economic chaos of the times and the lack of a dynasty popular and stable enough to evoke any enthusiasm. Yet in their freedom from wars, both external and internal, Africa Proconsularis and Numidia could, during the second half of the third century, be envied by almost every other province in the Empire. The revolt of barbarian tribes in 253/4, known only from inscriptions,[3] seems, from the location of these, to have taken place in the Djurdjura mountains of Mauretania Caesariensis, inhabited by the Quinquegentanei. The more serious revolt of 260, which involved both this tribe and the Bavares,[4] living at this period in the mountains between the Oued Sahel and Oued Kebir, was not entirely confined to Mauretania; in addition to actions in that part of the province later known as Mauretania Sitifensis fighting took place just over the Numidian border near Milev, and in some other area also on the borders of the two provinces.[5] It seems unlikely, however, that the more fertile parts of Numidia or the region of Sitifis itself were injured. Similarly, the

---

[1] SHA, *Vita Max.* 19; 'civitates subdidit, fana diripuit'.

[2] *C* 2170 (from Theveste); 'D.M.S. L. Aemilius Severinus qui et Phillyrio..., pro amore Romano quievit ab hoc Capeliano captus'.

[3] *C* 20827 (Ain du Dib); *C* 9045 (Auzia).

[4] *C* 9047 (Auzia).   [5] *C* 2615 (Lambaesis).

revolts of 287 and 297, though serious, were also confined to Mauretania. All these disturbances originated in mountainous districts which, though inside the boundaries of the Empire, were left in semi-independence. There seems to have been no trouble during this long period from the tribes outside the frontier except on the southern frontier of Mauretania Tingitana where pressure was sufficient to cause the abandonment of the frontier by Diocletian. This was, however, a relatively poor and unimportant part of Africa.

With the return of more settled conditions under Diocletian and Maximian, the repair of old buildings which had become ruinous and the erection of new works took place in many towns in Proconsularis, Byzacena and Numidia—an activity which had been almost entirely lacking in the preceding half century. It was paralleled to some extent in other parts of the Empire—in a well known passage Lactantius abused Diocletian for ruining the cities with his building programme.[1] In Africa at least a fair proportion of the work was carried out at the expense not of the cities but of private individuals. At Thugga a triumphal arch was erected to the two Augusti and the two Caesars,[2] and a private citizen restored the 'templum geni patriae' and distributed gifts to his fellow-decurions.[3] At Calama, a temple was restored by two citizens at a cost of 350,000 sesterces.[4] The decay in the same town in the previous reigns is indicated in an inscription[5] set up by a citizen who was also *curator reipublicae*; 'fortunam victricem cum simulacris victoriarum ex infrequenti et inculto loco in ista sede privato sumptu transtulit'. Thubursicu Numidarum saw the building of a temple to *Virtus Augusta* by private citizens.[6] These three towns were all of some importance in the province and had only reached colonial rank in the third century; they would naturally benefit most from any improvement in the situation. But there are also records of activity in some of the smaller towns, for instance Thignica,[7] Thala,[8] and Aunobaris.[9] In the *pagus* or *castellum* on the site of the present Hr. Ain Tella, the *seniores* repaired a temple of Mercury at their own expense.[10]

In Byzacena instances of similar activity occur. Sufetula, the most considerable town in the province, built a triumphal arch[11] and Segermes

---

[1] *De Mort. pers.* 7, 8–10.   [2] *C* 15516.   [3] *C* 26472.
[4] *C* 5333.   [5] *C* 5290.   [6] *ILAlg* 1241.
[7] *ILT* 1308.   [8] *AE* (1898), 48.   [9] *C* 27397.
[10] *C* 17327.   [11] *C* 11326.

a capitol.[1] Repairs to the theatre were carried out at the public expense at Ammaedara.[2] At Mididi occurs an inscription[3] which is worth quoting in full:

> Felicissimo saeculo DD.NN.C.Aureli Diocletiani pii felicis invicti Aug. et M. Aureli Valeri Maximiani pii felicis invicti Aug. quorum virtute ac providentia omnia in melius reformantur curia a solo extructa cum gradibus et porticibus continuis conferentibus universis curialibus civitat. Mididit. dedicante M.Aur.Aristobulo c.v.procos. Africae una cum Macrinio Sossiano c.v.leg.curante rem publicam Rupilio Pisoniano e.v.ordo splendidissimus epulum plebi prestantibus curialibus universis d.d.

This inscription indicates the fresh confidence which was felt in the African towns at this time. None of the inscriptions quoted so far go further than the usual 'beatissimo saeculo' in their dedications; but the phrase 'quorum virtute ac providentia omnia in melius reformantur' is new and seems to have been something more than a conventional honorific sentiment. It occurs again on the dedication of an arch of triumph, also at Mididi,[4] and on two inscriptions from Maktar.[5] These four instances are from the proconsulship of Aurelius Aristobulus, from 290 to 294, from which also survive no less than ten other records of repairs and construction of public buildings. Aristobulus seems to have had some sort of commission to carry out a general reconstruction of his province.[6] The greater part of his activity was in the south of Africa Proconsularis from which the new province of Byzacena was created shortly after his departure.[7]

It should be emphasized that we have no literary evidence concerning the state of urban prosperity in Africa at the beginning of the fourth century. Further, since few of the towns have been thoroughly excavated, we have to rely almost entirely on epigraphical evidence, and take into account both the inscriptions themselves and their distribution in time and place. What archaeological evidence there is does, however, support what inscriptions tell us of the building activity of this time. In the small town of Thibilis, in Numidia, which was apparently only made a *municipium* immediately before or during

---

[1] C 11167.   [2] C 11532.   [3] C 11774.
[4] C 608.   [5] C 624; AE (1946), 119.
[6] ILA 90, where he is called *auctor inventor et dedicator* of a public building. Other inscriptions: C 5290, 4645, 23413, 11768, 23657, 23658, 27816; ILAlg 2048; AE (1933), 60.
[7] Possibly in 295; see above, p. 1; and J. G. C. Anderson, JRS XXII (1932), 30.

the reign of Diocletian, two temples can be dated almost certainly to the end of the third century.[1] Repairs to a basilica at Thubursicu Numidarum were made about the same time.[2]

Numidia and the Mauretanias show fewer instances of rebuilding. Some of what was done was either of purely military significance, or represented the rebuilding of sites destroyed in the Moorish revolts of 289 or 297.[3] In most of those cases where damage had occurred through lack of attention in the past, the restoration was carried out at the instance of the governor.[4] An exception,[5] which also shows the stagnation of the preceding decades, was the building of two triumphal arches at Casae Nigrae, in southern Numidia. These had been promised by two decurions after an earthquake in 267, but the work was only undertaken by their sons in 286. Another exception is at Macomades, a town of some size, though somewhat isolated from the chief centres of population in Numidia. Here an arch of triumph was erected by two citizens of the town and statues of Victory provided by the town council on the occasion of the vicennalia of Diocletian and Maximian.[6]

In the matter of simple dedications to the rulers, usually with the conventional phrase 'devotus numini maiestatique eorum', the numbers found in the western provinces of Africa slightly exceed those of Proconsularis and Byzacena. Yet here the same distinction as in the public works is apparent. In Numidia and the Mauretanias it is in most cases the governor alone who makes the dedication, while in Proconsularis and Byzacena the initiative comes generally from the *ordo* of the various towns. This is explained by the fact that the Numidian and Mauretanian cities were usually of military origin and throughout their history more dependent on the activity of the governor and the army.[7] For instance, the persons chosen as *patroni* by the cities of these provinces were almost always the provincial governors, while in Africa Proconsularis the majority were members of provincial aristocracy.

Below are two tables giving the total numbers of inscriptions from the various provinces recording (A) the construction or repair of public buildings and works, excluding those of a military character, and (B)

---

[1] Gsell and Joly, *Khamissa, Mdaurouch, Announa*, 67–70.   [2] *Ibid.* 73.

[3] *AE* (1942/3), 84, building of a *centenarium* at Aqua Viva; *C* 20836, rebuilding of Rapidum.

[4] E.g. *C* 4224 (Verecunda), *C* 2660 (Lambaesis).

[5] *C* 2480, 2481.   [6] *C* 4764.

[7] T. R. S. Broughton, *The Romanization of Africa Proconsularis*, 126 ff.

dedications to the emperors and their families. These tables cover the period from the death of Gordian III to the Vandal conquest. Only those inscriptions which can definitely be dated are included. Reasons have already been given for the legitimacy of using the inscriptions statistically in the argument which follows. Tripolitania has been excluded since most of the inscriptions from that province are from one city, Lepcis Magna.

A. BUILDINGS AND REPAIRS

	244–84	284–306	306–37	337–63	363–83	383–429
Byzacena	1	18	3	2	3	1
Proconsularis	6	21	10	12	41	17
Numidia	6	8	2	1	21	6
Mauret. Sitif.	2	2	1	1	2	2
Mauret. Caes.	2	3	0	1	1	0

B. DEDICATIONS

	244–84	284–306	306–37	337–63	363–83	383–429
Byzacena	5	6	5	3	5	0
Proconsularis	37	23	21	10	21	9
Numidia	25	29	20	10	4	0
Mauret. Sitif.	2	7	7	3	0	0
Mauret. Caes.	5	8	2	0	0	0

Some idea of the revival of building under the Tetrarchy has been given. The table A shows that over this period of twenty years, four times as many records of such activity exist as over a period twice as long in the second half of the third century. The difference in Byzacena is even greater. When we reach the reign of Constantine, however, there is a considerable decline, especially in Numidia and Byzacena, where town life was less widespread and less firmly rooted than in Proconsularis. Two main reasons may be given for this. The first and chief one is the pressure on the *curiales*. This will be more thoroughly discussed later;[1] but it may be said here that the restoration of order by Diocletian and its maintenance by Constantine were dearly bought. To the upper classes in the towns the success of Diocletian must at first have appeared a blessing. The times of irregular and increasing exactions to meet some new emergency seemed to be over; a reformed currency was of greater benefit to them than to almost any other section of the

[1] See below, pp. 47 ff.

population. On the other hand, the rigid organization which he perfected meant the stricter collection of all taxes and closer supervision of the public functions of the *curiales*. From this time onwards the flow of laws dealing with this class and its attempts to escape its burdens becomes a flood, as may be seen from the enormous figure of 192 constitutions in the Theodosian Code[1] as well as numerous Novellae. So the impetus to public spirit in the towns given by the years of moderate prosperity and security under the Tetrarchy declined as the freedom of the *curiales* became more and more restricted.

The second reason must naturally be the measures taken by Maxentius against the wealthy classes. Even if we assume that material destruction was not great—there is no archaeological evidence of it having been so; and in any case the wealth of the cities was almost entirely in the land—the event was a shock of confidence. Inscriptions show that Constantine took the opportunity offered by the Africans' hatred of Maxentius to stress his own liberating activity. This propaganda of Constantine was indeed general in the West,[2] but as Africa was the most fertile field for it, so it provides the most striking examples. Cirta, the largest city in Numidia, had been ruined by Maxentius for its support of Alexander. Constantine rebuilt it, gave it his own name, and made it the provincial capital. The official viewpoint was represented in honorific dedications made to the emperor by the governors of Numidia and *rationales Numidiae et Mauretaniarum* between 315 and 320; he was referred to as 'fundator pacis, virtute, felicitate, pietate praestans',[3] as 'perpetuae securitatis ac libertatis auctor',[4] and as 'restitutor libertatis et conservator terrarum orbis'.[5] The most impressive was dedicated to him as 'triumphatori omnium gentium ac domitori universarum factionum qui libertatem tenebris servitutis oppressam sua felici victoria nova luce inluminavit....'.[6] Two inscriptions[7] from Lambaesis in a similar vein probably date from the same time, as also one from Uchi Maius in Africa Proconsularis.[8]

In 324 dedications were set up at Carthage and Utica, the most important cities in the proconsular province, which seem to have a more

[1] *Cod. Theod.* XII. I.

[2] Alföldi, *The Conversion of Constantine and Pagan Rome*, 63, 64.

[3] *C* 7008. [4] *C* 7005. [5] *C* 7010. [6] *C* 7006.

[7] *C* 2721, 18261.

[8] *C* 15451; 'domino triumfi libertatis et nostro restitutori invictis laboribus suis privatorum et publicae libertatis'.

direct object than celebration of the defeat of Licinius. In the first of these, the proconsul Maecilius Hilarianus refers to Constantine as 'instaurator atque amplificator universorum operum';[1] the other, set up by the same proconsul, runs: 'conditori adque amplificatori totius orbis Romani sui ac singularum quarumque civitatum statum adque ornatum liberalitate clementiae suae augenti. . . Constantino Aug. . . . .'[2] Whether the proconsul is speaking for himself or for the inhabitants of these places it is clear that Constantine was regarded, or wished to be regarded, as a restorer of the African cities.

Some public work was certainly carried out at private expense, including considerable repairs to the Old Forum at Thubursicu Numidarum by the grammarian Nonius Marcellus.[3] The persistence of paganism is shown by the rebuilding of a ruined temple of Mercury at Avitta Bibba at the instance of the proconsul in 337/8.[4]

The period from 337 to 363, comprising the reigns of Constans, Constantius II, and Julian, shows roughly the same amount of rebuilding which similarly is almost entirely confined to Africa Proconsularis. On the other hand, the greater part took place in the last few years of Constantius' reign or in that of Julian. At Thubursicu Numidarum in 361/2, a Forum Novum was repaired, or more probably built and decorated;[5] an arch also was built[6] and the old forum repaired.[7] This work was carried out by Atilius Theodotus, legate of the proconsul Q. Clodius Hermogenianus Olybrius, a member of one of the most powerful noble families of the fourth century. The proconsul was also responsible for the restoration of a triumphal arch at Theveste,[8] and a *tabularium* at Bulla Regia.[9]

A point of great interest arises from a study of dedications to the emperor made in Numidia between 337 and 363. Of the ten so far discovered, nine celebrate Julian who only reigned two years (361–3). Further, those which are complete enough show that the dedications were usually made by the town councils and not by the governor, as had been most common before. Of these inscriptions two explicitly celebrate Julian the restorer of the old religion, and indicate the strength of paganism in the cities at this time—from Thibilis[10] 'restitutor

---

[1] *C* 12524. The inscription is unfortunately mutilated, but this much is certain.
[2] *C* 1179.   [3] *C* 4878.   [4] *C* 12272.
[5] *ILAlg* 1229, 1247, 1274, 1276, etc.   [6] *ILAlg* 1285.
[7] *ILAlg* 1275.   [8] *C* 16505.   [9] *C* 25521.
[10] *AE* (1893), 87.

sacrorum' and from Casae[1] 'restitutor libertatis et Romanae religionis'. Also noteworthy is a dedication to him at Lambaesis[2] with the words 'providentissimo et cum orbe suo reddita libertate'. This is exactly the same phraseology as that used in a dedication at the same place to Constantine[3] after the defeat of Maxentius. This must surely be more than a coincidence, and probably represents a deliberate affront to the Catholics. There is evidence, quite apart from these inscriptions, to show that there would be nothing surprising in an outburst of pagan confidence resulting from Julian's religious policy. Notwithstanding the rapid advance of Christianity in the third century it is certain that most town councils, and even some whole towns were still almost entirely pagan. Thibilis, the source of one of these strictly pagan inscriptions, a small town thoroughly excavated, shows no Christian inscriptions before the sixth century; none at all were found at the larger town of Thubursicu Numidarum.[4] Paganism was still strong in other cities in the time of Augustine.[5] It can hardly be doubted also that the particular enthusiasm in Numidia was connected with Julian's grant of freedom of worship to the Donatists, the stronger of the two Christian Churches in the province, who had been persecuted in the preceding reigns. To hail an emperor as a restorer of liberty was indeed often—but not always[6]—a piece of mere rhetoric, but Constantius was hardly one of the short-lived tyrants whose fall usually brought forth such flattery. Nor is there anything unlikely in an association of pagan and Donatist sentiment; an instance is known of Roman officials, undoubtedly pagan, looking on while Donatists offered violence to Catholics.[7] That Donatism as much as paganism was responsible for the feeling which produced these inscriptions may be indicated in a negative way by the fact that only four occur in Africa Proconsularis where the Catholics were supreme. Lastly, after the extreme rigour of Constantius' financial policy, Julian's attempt to revive urban life and ease the condition of the *curiales* seemed to promise more than eventually transpired.[8]

---

[1] C 18529.
[2] AE (1916), 11; other dedications to Julian in Numidia are AE (1937), 145, (1916), 20, (1909), 232, (1949), 134; C 4771, 2387.
[3] C 2721.   [4] Gsell and Joly, *op. cit.*
[5] Aug. *Epp.* 16 (Madauros), 80 (Sufes), 90 (Calama).
[6] The removal of Maxentius by Constantine was undoubtedly beneficial.
[7] Optatus, II. 18; see below, p. 95.   [8] See below, pp. 52 ff.

The extraordinary effort made between 364 (accession of Valentinian I) and 383 (death of Gratian) to carry out repairs in a large number of cities both in Africa Proconsularis and in Numidia is one of the most interesting facts revealed by the epigraphy of North Africa. In the former province, towns of varying importance are among those where such work was carried out, from Carthage[1] down to the insignificant Castellum Biracsaccarensium,[2] and numerous places, the old names of which have not been preserved.[3] Repairs were carried out not only by the town councils but also by private persons, often those who held or had held the position of *curator reipublicae*. Two examples from Thugga[4] show dedications to have been made to celebrate the holding of municipal office—an occurrence common enough in the second century, but in general quite out of place in the fourth, when such office was considered, and usually was, an oppressive burden. The latter of these inscriptions also records the giving of a feast to the townspeople, in the old manner. An example completer than most is transcribed here as indicating the usual style of such inscriptions.[5]

Pro tanta securitate (temporum) DD.NN. Valentiniani (et Valentis perpetuo)rum Au(gg. thermas) aestivas, olim splen(did.) coloniae (nostrae ornamentum sed tot re)tro annis ruinarum deformas parietibusque omnium soliorum ita corruptis ut gravibus damnis adficerent, nunc omni idonitate constructas at cultu splendido decoratas, sed et patinas ampliato aeris pondere omni idonitate firmissimas, proconsulatu Publi Ampeli v.c. Octavio Privatiano v.c. legato Numidiae Caec. Pontilius Paulinus ff.pp. patronus coloniae curator reipublicae pecunia publica perfecit.... [The rest of the inscription is mutilated.]

The 'securitas temporum', 'felicitas temporum' and 'aureum saeculum' of these reigns are featured in many inscriptions. Public baths were the buildings most commonly restored.[6] After half a century of government by Christian emperors we find repairs to a temple at Thibursicu Bure[7] and possibly at Madauros[8] where the temple of Fortuna was being used as a market. Towns where several

---

[1] *C* 12536.   [2] *C* 23849.
[3] E.g. Hr. Baia, Hr. Tout-el-Kaya.
[4] *C* 26568 (*ILA* 533) 'pro honore flamonii perp.' (376); *C* 26569, 'ob honorem duoviratus' (379–83).
[5] *ILAlg* 2101, Madauros (364).
[6] E.g. at Calama (*C* 5335), Madauros (*ILAlg* 2101), Tubernuc (*C* 948).
[7] *C* 1447.   [8] *ILAlg* 2103.

restorations are recorded are Calama (baths,[1] amphitheatre,[2] theatre[3] and several other buildings of which the description is missing)[4] and Thugga.[5]

Much legislation on the subject took place in the reign of Valentinian, the chief points being the return of one third of the civic revenue specifically for maintenance of public buildings,[6] and the repeated orders against the undertaking of new building while unfinished or ruined work remained.[7] At such a time the attitude of governors was most important, for there can be little doubt they controlled all public works and had to give consent—or perhaps a stimulus—on each occasion.[8] The proconsul of Africa was not subordinate, save on a few special occasions, to the vicar of the African diocese. He was chosen by the praetorian prefect, usually from among the highest nobility at Rome. Of the governors in the period under review the most energetic, if we may judge from the inscriptions and in one case from an anecdote of Ammianus Marcellinus, were Festus Hymetius and Decimius Hilarianus Hesperius. The name of the former, who was a pagan though married to a Christian, appears on five inscriptions referring to building or rebuilding.[9] During his governorship in 366/7 a shortage of food occurred at Carthage and to alleviate distress he opened the granaries containing supplies destined for Rome and sold some of them. He was subsequently prosecuted on a charge of having kept some of the money, and exiled, though it seems clear that he was innocent.[10] He was not forgotten by his province; on his return to Rome after the death of Valentinian, the provincial council erected gilt statues of him in Carthage and Rome, an honour which had never been given to former proconsuls, with the thankful inscription:[11]

> ...ob insignia eius in rempublicam merita et ob depulsam ab eadem provincia famis et inopiae vastitatem consiliis et provisionibus, et quod caste in eadem provincia integreque versatus est, quod neque aequitati in cognoscendo neque justitiae defuerit, quod studium sacerdotii provinciae restituerit ut nunc a conpetitoribus adpetatur quod antea formidini fuerit....

The clause concerning the position of the *sacerdotium provinciae* is of interest. Mention has been made of inscriptions from this period which

---

[1] *C* 5335.
[2] *C* 5336.
[3] *ILAlg* 260.
[4] *C* 5339; *ILAlg* 259.
[5] *ILT* 1500; *C* 26568.
[6] See below, p. 52.
[7] *Cod. Theod.* xv. 1. 15 (365).
[8] See below, p 44.
[9] *C* 5335, 5336, 1782, 23863; *ILAlg* 2102.
[10] Amm. Marc. xxviii. 1. 17–19.
[11] *CIL* vi, 1736.

refer to civil functions as *honores*. These could be explained on the grounds that they only repeated the official terminology which continued to refer to such *honores* long after all possible truth in the term had vanished. This explicit reference on an inscription to the desirability of a position held by *ex-curialibus* is somewhat different. One can only be intrigued at wondering what measures Hymetius took to restore the prestige of the *sacerdotales* to an extent that was still effective ten years afterwards.

Hilarianus Hesperius, son of the poet Ausonius, governed the province in 376, the first of the four years when the poet's family monopolized the great offices in the west.[1] Eight public works are recorded from his proconsulship, of which he initiated four.[2]

In Numidia, where records of municipal building activity between the end of the Tetrarchy and the reign of Julian are almost entirely lacking, over half[3] the works undertaken between 363 and 383 are associated with the name of Publilius Ceionius Caecina Albinus, governor between 364 and 367. In the fourth and early fifth centuries, the Ceionii played almost as considerable a part in public life as the Anicii. The Emperor Julian was, through his mother, connected with the family which, unlike the Anicii, remained on the male side strongly pagan into the fifth century. It had already provided several governors for the African provinces and was to produce others.[4] Albinus subsequently became one of the ornaments of Roman pagan society and is one of the protagonists in Macrobius' *Saturnalia*. These Ceionii may perhaps have been of African origin. Albinus restored a building at Mascula,[5] 'ad splendorem tam patriae quam provinciae'. The writer of the Life of Clodius Albinus traces their descent from him. This can hardly be genuine,[6] nor can the birthplace of Clodius be certainly fixed at Hadrumetum as the Life says,[7] but at least it can be said that an African origin of the family was held by the circle which produced the

---

[1] Symmachus, ed. Seeck, p. cvii.

[2] *C* 1219 (Vaga), 17519 (Calama), 25632 (Simitthus), 25845 (Hr. el Baharine); the others, *C* 14346, 26568; *ILA* 275; *ILAlg* 257.

[3] *C* 6975, 19502 (Cirta); 20156, *AE* (1911), 110, (1946), 107 (Cuicul); *C* 2656, 18229 (Lambaesis); 2242, *AE* (1911), 217 (Mascula); *C* 19852 (Rusicade); 2388 (Thamugadi); *AE* (1909), 222 (Hr. el Abiod); *C* 18701 (Ksur-el-Āhmar).

[4] E.g. C. Ceionius Rufus, *procos. Afr. c.* 308; Ceionius Italicus, *cons. Numid.* 343; A. Ceionius Julianus, *vic. Afr.* 381; C. Decius Albinus, *cons. Numid. c.* 388–92.

[5] *AE* (1911), 217.   [6] Seeck in *P-W* III, 1858.

[7] *PIR* II², 281.

Augustan history, with whom the Ceionii, influential pagans throughout the fourth century, were doubtless connected. The father of Albinus had an estate in Africa Proconsularis.[1]

His activity is found in all the larger towns of Numidia. At Cuicul, three works were undertaken, one of which was a new basilica.[2] At Mascula, Lambaesis and Constantine his name appears twice in each place as the originator of repairs.[3] New granaries were built at the port of Rusicade to serve the needs both of Rome and the provincials.[4] The usual style of these Numidian inscriptions opened with such a phrase as 'pro magnificentia saeculi' or 'pro beatitudine saeculi'.[5] At Mascula, Albinus introduced a note which, though perhaps connected with the possibility of his African origin, doubtless reflected imperial thought about this period of reconstruction:[6]

Aureis ubique temporibus DD.NN. Valentiniani et Valentis perpetuorum Augg., statum desperata recipiunt, amissa renovantur, ruinarum deformitatem decor novitatis excludit. Iamdudum igitur thermarum aestivalium fabulam factam depellens faciemque restituens Publilius Caeionius Caecina Albinus v.c. consularis ad splendorem tam patriae quam provinciae restituit. . . .

It may be admitted that the Ceionii were much addicted to having their names inscribed upon monuments; Lampadius, *praefectus urbi* in 365, father of Albinus, was the object of derision at Rome for the number of buildings he claimed to have founded.[7] The activity of Albinus in Numidia, however, is paralleled by that in Africa Proconsularis. His successors accomplished nothing so considerable, but there was steady activity during the next dozen years or so. The new basilica at Cuicul was decorated immediately after Albinus' governorship with two Victories by the strongly pagan governor Faventius, and a *porticus Gratiana* was built in the same city between 367 and 375. After the death of Gratian, however, in both Africa Proconsularis and Numidia public works became fewer and fewer and ceased entirely some years before the Vandal conquest.

Considerable fluctuations in the prosperity and public spirit of the African towns are thus clear from epigraphical evidence. These

[1] *C* 25990. [2] *AE* (1946), 383; *C* 20156; *AE* (1911), 110.
[3] *C* 2242; *AE* (1911), 217; *C* 2656, 18229, 6975, 19502.
[4] *C* 19852. [5] *C* 19852, 2388, 18701, 20156.
[6] *AE* (1911), 217. [7] Amm. Marc. XXVII. 3. 7.

fluctuations were due neither to invasions by barbarian tribes, nor to destruction in civil war, but to the different policies adopted by fourth-century emperors towards the *curiales*. Before going on to consider the numerous laws dealing with this subject, we must first consider the actual composition and duties of the *curiae*.

The composition of an African town council of moderate size in the fourth century is exactly known from the inscription[1] usually called the 'Album of Thamugadi', dated about 363. This inscription lists all the members of the *curia*, with their office, and the imperial officials stationed in the town. The following gives the number of each rank:

10 *viri clarissimi* (five of whom were patrons of the city).
2 *viri perfectissimi* (one of whom was also *flamen perpetuus*).
2 *sacerdotales* (one of whom was a patron, the other *flamen perpetuus*).
1 *curator reipublicae* (also *flamen perpetuus*).
2 *duoviri* (one was also *augur*, the other *flamen perpetuus*).
32 *flamines perpetui* (two of whom were *exactores*).[2]

4 *pontifices*.	3 *quaestores*.
3 *augures*.	15 *duoviralici*.
2 *aediles*.	

At least 6 *aedilici non excusati*.
 ,, 3 *quaestorici non excusati*.
 ,, 30 *non honores functi excusati*.
 ,, 43 *non honores functi non excusati*.
 ,, 7   ?
11 *clerici*.

The imperial officials were:

5	serving in the office of the vicar of Africa.			
37	,,	,,	,,	*consularis* of Numidia.
23	,,	,,	,,	*praefectus annonae*.
5	,,	,,	,,	*rationalis provinciae*.

The *viri clarissimi* and *viri perfectissimi* may have been persons who had passed through all the grades in the council and obtained by some means the title giving them freedom from further burdens, or citizens who had reached positions carrying these titles in the imperial service and now held a place of honour in the community without any duties to perform. Those who were patrons were not necessarily inhabitants of the city or even Africa; for instance, at the head of the *viri clarissimi*,

---

[1] *C* 2403, 17903, and a new fragment, with discussion by L. Leschi, in *Revue des études anciennes*, L (1948), 71 ff. See also Mommsen, *Ges. Schrift*. VIII, 312.
[2] See below, p. 53.

and thus of the Album itself, comes the name of Vulcacius Rufinus, patron of the city, a relative of the Emperor Julian, who had governed the province of Numidia about 340.[1] In the first centuries of the Empire, the municipal *patroni* had had the duty of looking after the interests of their client towns at Rome, if they were influential enough, or with the provincial governor if they were of only local importance. With the later decline in the prosperity of the cities, the patrons were undoubtedly more concerned with protecting their clients against oppression by governors or officials; many governors were in fact themselves chosen as patrons by the cities, perhaps in the hope that they would behave in an appropriate fashion. There is nothing to show when Rufinus became patron, but at the date of the inscription, he could have been a useful person owing to his imperial connexion. None of the other *patroni* are known. The *vir perfectissimus* who was also *flamen perpetuus* may have been one of those who had obtained the higher rank without going through the *curia* or other proper formality and was subsequently recalled to fulfil his functions.[2] The *sacerdotales*, who had originally been priests of the imperial cult but were now usually lawyers, were persons who had completed their municipal burdens and had been chosen by the *concilium provinciae* to serve in that body for a period as yet uncertain. *Sacerdotales* were undoubtedly wealthy men and at a slightly later date were almost as high in the social scale as the *clarissimi*.[3]

The first of the members of the *curia* (or *ordo* as it is alternatively called) who has an effective function to perform is the *curator rei-publicae*. This office was by far the most important in the municipal constitution, and its development in Africa is well known. The earliest *curatores* in the Empire as a whole date from the reign of Trajan. They were appointed to supervise or reorganize the affairs of cities which had got into financial difficulties, and appear first in Italy and Gaul. As a general rule the *curator* had charge of only one city[4] and his chief task was to prevent it getting into debt through over-building or corruption. At first, the benefits of the institution probably outweighed the inherent disadvantage, which was the deadening effect on local initiative of control by the central government. It must be admitted that the

[1] Pallu de Lessert, *op. cit.* 323.
[2] *Cod. Theod.* XII. I. 42 (354). See below, p. 49, for an example of a *vir clarissimus* performing municipal duties.
[3] *Cod. Theod.* XVI. 5. 52 (412).
[4] But see *ILA* 44 for a *curator* of four towns in Africa Proconsularis.

inhibiting activity of the *curatores* can only be inferred, not proved. The first *curator* who can be dated in an African province is from the reign of Septimius Severus,[1] nearly a century after the institution of the office; in view of the very large number of inscriptions recording *curatores* in Africa,[2] it is unlikely that this is far from the true date of their introduction. The cities were probably so prosperous throughout the second century that even if some had got into difficulty the despatch of a *curator* would have been an unnecessary attention.

The number of communities which had a *curator* increased steadily during the third century. They would certainly have become necessary in many cases as a result of the general insecurity. A more rapid increase occurred in the reigns of Diocletian and Constantine; this can be accounted for by the policies of those emperors towards centralization. The process continued right up to the end of Roman rule in Africa; over sixty different communities are recorded as having them.[3]

At the beginning of the fourth century there were considerable changes both in the kind of persons made *curatores* and in their work. *Curatores* of both senatorial and equestrian rank were the general rule up to the time of Diocletian. Several are known to have come from outside Africa, but in some cases African *curatores* served in their own province, though not in their own cities. From the reign of Diocletian it became increasingly common for a *curator* to come from among the highest officers—usually *flamines perpetui*—of his own city.[4] One of the *flamines* named in the Album became *curator reipublicae* within a year or so and was later chosen as patron of the city.[5] There had been one or two examples of local *curatores* in the early third century, but from Constantine's time it became the rule; no more *curatores* of senatorial rank occur after his reign. The law of 331[6] which permitted *curiales* to become *curatores* only after fulfilling all their prescribed duties is dealing with what, in Africa, must have been a common occurrence.

Thus, from being an instrument of control by the centre, the *curator* became, in Africa at least, the highest rank in the city councils. That it was a real office and not a *munus* is shown by the law quoted, and by an

---

[1] *ILA* 131 (A.D. 196).
[2] See C. Lucas, 'Notes on the *curatores reipublicae* of Roman Africa', *JRS* xxx (1940), 55 ff.
[3] C. Lucas, *ibid.*
[4] C. Lucas, *ibid.* 62.
[5] *AE* (1913), 25; *C* 2388.
[6] *Cod. Theod.* XII. 1. 20.

inscription from Neapolis, in Proconsularis.[1] In this case a man who had completed his career as a *navicularius*, an occupation which gave complete immunity from curial burdens, was afterwards *curator* of his city. It seems probable also that the office was elective. In the Album, the *curator reipublicae* comes at the head of the municipal offices and not among the *administratores*, or persons holding imperial positions or honours. This inferior position shows that it was a municipal, not an imperial office, in accordance with a law giving precedence in the municipalities to the latter.[2]

The work of the *curatores*, so far as we know it, became more restricted. Control over public building remained a considerable part of their office; but during the fourth century it was usually the provincial governor who was responsible for initiating public building, and the *curator* who had the purely executive task of carrying it out.[3] Thus the governor impinged on an important part of the work of the local councils, and defined the policy to be followed in his province. There is, however, evidence that the *curatores* in some cities carried out the decrees of Diocletian relative to the persecution of the Christians. Instances of this occur at Cirta, Rusicade and Tigisi.[4] This duty of seeking out the Christians and requiring their obedience was carried out in other cities by *duoviri*, the highest municipal magistrates; it would appear that in Numidia at least the powers of these magistrates were being taken over by the *curatores*.

After the *curator reipublicae* come the various other offices just as they were in the second century when town life was flourishing. The *flamines perpetui* were chosen as priests for life of one of the deified emperors presumably when they were at the beginning of the municipal *cursus*.[5] In view of their large number, the attitude of the Church,[6] and the smallness at this late date of the burden which such an office would carry, they doubtless had other and heavier charges to fulfil as well. Cases are fairly common, including possibly one from Thamugadi

---

[1] *C* 969.

[2] Ulpian, *Dig.* L. 3. 2; 'in albo decurionum in municipio nomina ante scribi oportet eorum qui dignitates principis iudicio consecuti sunt, postea eorum, qui tantum municipalibus honoribus functi sunt'.

[3] References in C. Lucas, *loc. cit.* 71, 72.

[4] Appendix I to Optatus, *CSEL* XXVI, 186; Aug. *contra Cresconium* III. 27. 30.

[5] Mommsen, *Ges. Schrift.* VIII, 318.

[6] E.g. Canons I and 2 of the Council of Elvira, 305.

itself,[1] of Christians holding the office. It is most likely that the *pontifices* had charge of the official cult and the management of temple property. There is no evidence as to which of the many different burdens was allotted to the ranks within the *curiae*.

Below these officers of higher rank come thirty men at least who are termed *non honores functi excusati*—persons who were excused municipal burdens though they had not been through them. Since they come so low in precedence, they cannot have been of any high rank which brought immunity, nor can they have been *officiales*, who are listed later. There were, however, various professions members of which obtained exemption chiefly because the profession itself was considered a sufficient public duty. Typical examples were the *navicularii*,[2] who were very important in Africa, being responsible for the shipment of food to Rome; teachers of all grades and doctors;[3] and merchants (*negotiatores*), who paid special taxes.[4] Veterans were also exempt, and *curiales* who had joined the Palatine service, the officials of which were subordinate to the greater officers of state.[5] (*Curiales* were forbidden to enter the *officia* of less exalted persons such as vicars and provincial governors.)[6] On the other hand, we have no evidence of compulsion being applied to the *excusati* to join the *curia* even though their position there would be purely honorary. We are left with the conclusion that, in the particular case under discussion and presumably in other African cities, many of them joined through entirely voluntary motives, or at least because public opinion required it of men of their class. In either case, however burdensome the position of *curialis* had become, it was still not entirely without honour.[7] Below the *excusati* come over forty persons referred to as *non honores functi non excusati*, that is, persons who were not exempt from service and had not yet performed it. These were perhaps younger men who had just joined the *curia* but had not yet started on the municipal *cursus*.

---

[1] *AE* (1913), 25 (dated *c.* 366). This *tabula patronatus* given to the former *curator reipublicae* and *flamen perpetuus*, Aelius Julianus, bears the Christian monogram; but this could be a later addition. For other Christian *flamines perpetui*, perhaps of Vandal date, see *C* 450, 10516.

[2] *Cod. Theod.* XIII. 5. 5 (326). [3] *Cod. Theod.* XIII. 3. 1 and 2 (321, 326).

[4] *Cod. Theod.* XIII. 1. 1 (356; but the practice was much older).

[5] E.g. the praetorian prefect, or the *magister officiorum*.

[6] *Cod. Theod.* XII. 1. 67 (365), 100 (383).

[7] Cf. also the inscriptions quoted above in which the holding of municipal office is regarded as an honour.

The last feature of interest in this important inscription is the appearance of eleven *clerici*. These are certainly Christian clergy, the legal definition of the word having been given by Constantine.[1] By this same law, the clergy were given complete immunity from all burdens, an immunity which had to be confirmed several times in later years.[2] At the same time, it was forbidden for *curiales* or their sons to take orders, and laid down that only the poor could do so.[3] This regulation was, however, certainly often evaded.[4] Thus the position remained until the end of the reign of Constantius. In 359/60 a law was promulgated ordering merchants and landowners who had become clergy (*clerici possessores*) to fulfil their obligations to the *fiscus*;[5] but clergy of curial rank were still immune from personal service though they might have to hand over part of their property.[6] Julian took away clerical immunity and ordered those who had enjoyed it to return to their *curiae* and carry out their civic duties.[7] The Album of Thamugadi shows that this was put into effect; indeed, the enthusiasm already noted[8] of some African towns for Julian's pagan ideals would ensure its prompt execution. That there is no erasure on the stone at Thamugadi may indicate that clerical immunity was not at once restored. In 364 Valentinian and Valens laid down that clergy could only be immune if they provided a relative as substitute or made over sufficient property to their *curia*.[9] This was the principle which, in the main, governed clerical immunity during the rest of the century.

There can be no doubt that the *curiae* of other cities throughout Africa were similarly organized in the fourth century. Mention has been made of the general rule by which *curatores* were chosen from among the *flamines perpetui*;[10] the only other municipal office to appear in inscriptions is that of *duovir*. This is only natural in that the lower offices had no connexion with public works and dedications.

[1] *Cod. Theod.* XVI. 2. 2 (319); 'qui divino cultui ministeria religionis inpendunt, id est hi, qui clerici appellantur, ab omnibus omnino muneribus excusentur'. And cf. Eusebius, *Hist. Eccl.* X. 7.

[2] *Cod. Theod.* XVI. 2. 7 (330) and XVI. 2. 9 (349).

[3] *Cod. Theod.* XVI. 2. 3 (320).

[4] *Cod. Theod.* XVI. 2. 6 (326).

[5] *Cod. Theod.* XVI. 2. 15.

[6] *Cod. Theod.* XII. 1. 49.

[7] *Cod. Theod.* XVI. 1. 50; Julian, *Ep.* 39; Ensslin, *Klio* XXIII (1923), 41.

[8] See above p. 36.

[9] *Cod. Theod.* XII. 1. 59.

[10] See above, p. 43.

We turn now to a consideration of the duties of the *curiales* and the enormous amount of legislation concerning them. The members of the *curiae*, in addition to the responsibility for the purely local affairs of the community which had always been theirs, were now in effect unpaid servants of the imperial administration. The local responsibilities were heavy enough; they included the finances of the communities and the usual tasks of local government such as the maintenance of roads, bridges and public buildings. Heavy expenditure on amusements for the people was prescribed by law or custom for certain of the offices in the *curia*. These might have been borne with little complaint or even with pride in prosperous times, as the correspondingly heavy expenses were borne by the members of the senate at Rome; what chiefly made the struggle between the *curiales* and the imperial administration so intense was the determination of the former to escape from the load of personal responsibility for the numerous charges laid on them by the latter. The chief of these was the assessment of taxes in their cities and surrounding territories and their collection, with responsibility for any deficit. The *curiales* had also to maintain the imperial post service, arrange the supplies of the army, and in Africa at least make the initial collection of the *annona*.[1]

The formidable number of laws restricting the freedom of the *curiales* is well known and is largely responsible for the universal agreement on the extremely depressed state of this class in the later Empire. The whole purpose of these laws was to prevent the *curiales* from leaving their position in society, at least until they had completed some twenty-five years' service and gone through the various ranks in the *curiae*. It was a political commonplace of the time to regard this as essential to the state.[2] Yet it has not been sufficiently observed that it was not merely the personal burden of the *curiales* which prompted their flight, but also legitimate ambition. It was from this class that the bulk of officials of both higher and lower grades and the liberal professions had for centuries been recruited. The establishment during the third century[3] of hereditary obligation to the *curia* meant that young men, whether wealthy or not, would be debarred from any social advancement. If a man remained in the *curia*, he could only hope

[1] See below, p. 60.
[2] *Cod. Theod.* XII. 1. 32 (341); 'reipublicae incommodum est curias hominum paucitate languescere'.
[3] Stein, *Geschichte des spätrömischen Reiches*, I, 71.

to reach the duovirate and at length pass into the class of *principales*, to whom a privilege of freedom from torture was given.[1]

In 336, *curiales* or their sons who had become officials were to return to their towns, unless they were in the Palatine service.[2] Three laws addressed to Africa about this time show curial desertions to have been common there. One directs the vicar to order men who had obtained —not necessarily corruptly—the titles of *ex-comite* and *ex-praeside* which released them from the *curia* to carry out the municipal duties which they had previously omitted.[3] Another[4] refers to the *curia* of Carthage itself which had lost many of its members through acquirement by bribery of these and other titles which gave immunity. This is the first of many laws dealing with this abuse and indicates not only the corruption of the administrative system, but the determination of the municipal aristocracy to free themselves (and their descendants) from profitless labour. In 353 *ex-comitibus* and *ex-praesidibus* who had belonged to the *curia* of Carthage were ordered to complete their municipal functions.[5] In Africa also desertion from the *curia* to the army had been going on for so long—despite numerous laws against it—that even veterans who had originally been liable for curial service were recalled to their towns.[6]

Still more attractive to the *curiales* was entry into the senatorial order. This order as a whole had long ceased to have any connexion with the exercise of senatorial functions; for many, particularly in the provinces, membership was merely a social distinction, implying either the possession of considerable landed property or the tenure of some honorary, if expensive, position.[7] But for its members all the highest civil offices in the Empire were reserved; and if progress within its ranks was exceedingly costly at the beginning of a career, pride in its tradition or hope of future power made for general acquiescence.[8] It need hardly be said that quite apart from the increasing power of the class, often outside the law,[9] it possessed important privileges the most important of which was that of complete exemption from municipal burdens.[10]

---

[1] *Cod. Theod.* XII. 1. 61 (364).
[2] *Cod. Theod.* XII. 1. 22.
[3] *Cod. Theod.* XII. 1. 26 (338).
[4] *Cod. Theod.* XII. 1. 27 (339).
[5] *Cod. Theod.* XII. 1. 41.
[6] *Cod. Theod.* XII. 1. 45 (358).
[7] Dill, *Roman Society in the last Century of the Western Empire*, 249.
[8] E.g. the orator Symmachus paid enormous sums for his son's praetorship. See also Stein, *op. cit.* 50.   [9] See below, p. 66.   [10] *Cod. Theod.* VI. 3. 2, 3.

The earliest law dealing with the matter is dated to 340,[1] though naturally there may have been earlier ones. It is interesting that the recipient of this constitution was the city council of Cirta, in Numidia, and perhaps answers a complaint from it. The principle is laid down that no one could enter the senatorial order before completing curial burdens. This was repeated in 353,[2] though it would seem that those who had already entered the senate could remain; but in 361 it was ordered that they should return to their cities unless they had held the praetorship which was a very expensive burden.[3] Those who wished to enter the order had to prove to the governor of their province that they had completed their municipal duties.[4] Sons borne after the entry of their father into the order were made liable to the expensive honour of the quaestorship or praetorship, but excused from curial service. Yet this law was soon[5] changed; *curiales* who had become senators before completing their *munera* could keep their new rank provided they performed their curial duties as well. An inscription[6] from Cuicul in Numidia probably illustrates this. Between 367 and 375, Rutilius Saturninus, *vir clarissimus*, paid for the building of a basilica 'pro editione muneris debiti'. Provincial governors and even the *curiae* themselves connived at desertions.[7]

The flow of laws aimed at preventing every conceivable method by which the *curiales* could escape continued. Yet enough has been given here to show that at least till the time of Valentinian the legislation was chiefly to prevent *curiales* deserting their positions for the higher ranks in society, and thus the objective of the *curiales* was not merely to escape from a very burdensome, dangerous and in general unhonoured position, but to further what were, after all, legitimate ambitions. We may note that Augustine's father Patricius was of curial rank at Thagaste;[8] when Augustine showed his promise as a student, Patricius went to great expense to send him to Carthage for better instruction—and would have been unable to do this without the help of a wealthy friend—in order that his son might have a career at law.[9] How it was that Augustine escaped being recalled to the *curia* on his father's death

---

[1] *Cod. Theod.* XII. 1. 29.   [2] *Cod. Theod.* XII. 1. 18.

[3] *Cod. Theod.* XII. 1. 48.   [4] *Cod. Theod.* XII. 1. 57 and 58 (364).

[5] *Cod. Theod.* XII. 1. 69 of uncertain date, but subsequent to *Cod. Theod.* XII. 1. 57. Mommsen gives the alternatives 365, 368, 370 or 373.

[6] *C* 8324; see also *C* 20156.   [7] *Cod. Theod.* XII. 1. 71 (370).

[8] Possidius, *Vita Aug.* 1.   [9] Aug. *Confess.* II. 3. 5; *contra Acad.* II. 3.

is unknown; perhaps he had an elder brother; yet Augustine inherited an estate from his father.[1] We know little of how deficiencies in the *curiae* were made up. Certainly the sons of veterans, who normally followed their fathers' calling, were brought into the *curia* if for reasons of health they could not serve in the army. Further, if a law of 342 addressed to the *comes orientis* was applicable in the Western provinces also, the possession of only twenty-five *jugera* of land compelled a man to become a *curialis*; Augustine refers to a certain Curma as 'curialis pauper, vix duumviralicius et simpliciter rusticanus'. The name is native, and the town, *municipium Tulliense*, in the region of Hippo Regius, was doubtless an insignificant place.[2] Obviously there was a great difference in the pressure of municipal burdens on such a small landowner and on a member of the *Karthaginis splendidissimae senatus*.[3] As was mentioned above,[4] achievement of higher rank by members of the *curia* of Carthage was twice specifically referred to in imperial constitutions; men who obtained the rank of *comes*, whether by merit or bribery, were unlikely to have been poor. Further, it may be deduced from the scale of penalties laid down for persistence in Donatism[5] that the *sacerdotales*, who were chosen from among the advocates who had fulfilled all their civic burdens, were generally as wealthy as members of the senatorial order. It was not till the end of the fourth century and the beginning of the fifth that *curiales*, despairing of advancement[6] and finally overcome by the exactions of the government and the abuses of the officials in face of the rapid disintegration of the Empire, fled in large numbers to positions lower in society. Most frequently, they put themselves under the patronage of some landowner powerful enough to prevent their being dragged back to the *curia*. This had been noticed during the reign of Julian[7] and again some ten years later.[8] After the end of the fourth century, those who sheltered the *curiales* were threatened with punishments of ever increasing severity, ending with burning alive.[9] The flight of *curiales* to a lower status was particularly common in Gaul, where the nobles seem to have

---

[1] Aug. *Ep.* 126. 7; Possidius, *Vita Aug.* 3.
[2] *Cod. Theod.* XII. 1–33; Aug. *de Cura pro mortuis agenda*, XII. 15; *CSEL* XLI, 644.
[3] *Cod. Theod.* XII. 1. 27.   [4] On p. 48.
[5] *Cod. Theod.* XVI. 15. 52 (412).
[6] *Cod Theod.* XII. 1. 183 (418) forbids them entry into the senatorial order.
[7] *Cod. Theod.* XII. 1. 50 (362).   [8] *Cod. Theod.* XII. 1. 76 (371).
[9] *Cod. Theod.* XII. 1. 179 (415).

reached a more powerful position than in other provinces; it was in Gaul that the lurid picture of society given by Salvian in the middle of the fifth century is set. There is a perfectly clear reason for this. The northern provinces had been subjected to increasingly numerous attacks by German tribes ever since the time of Julian. These culminated in the complete breakdown of the imperial defences in 406/7 and the devastation of Italy, Gaul and Spain by the Goths and Vandals. That the *curiales* survived as a class at all is surprising. The tax collectors took little account of the losses caused by such calamities. Almost as bad as the destruction of wealth by the barbarians was the oppression of the provincials by the army which was supposed to defend them.

It is well to remember that Africa did not suffer such disaster till the Vandal invasion in 429, and it is thus probable that the position of the *curiales* there at the turn of the century was not so desperate as that of their fellows the other side of the Mediterranean. Nevertheless it is clear that the evidence of the almost complete cessation of work on public buildings after *c.* 383 matches that of the increasingly severe laws against the *curiales* and confirms that roughly after the death of Gratian their position became rapidly worse.

While the laws designed to prevent *curiales* from leaving their places of residence continued, some efforts were made about the middle of the fourth century to alleviate the financial state of the cities and their *curiae*. It is noteworthy that the first step of this kind was taken by Constantius, whose general record in the provinces is adversely criticized by Ammianus.[1] He restored to the cities a quarter of the revenue which they had formerly obtained from their corporate property and which had been confiscated by some previous emperor. The condition was that the money should be used for maintaining fortifications.[2] Since this had always been a municipal responsibility, the new law was a considerable relief to the *curiales* who must have been personally responsible since the confiscation of municipal revenues. The law in question was addressed to the vicar of Africa, and the cities of this diocese seem to be particularly in view. It may be that the relief was confined to Africa and resulted from some special emergency. It is

---

[1] XXI. 16. 17.

[2] *Cod. Theod.* IV. 13. 5 (358); 'divalibus jussis addimus firmitatem et vectigalium quartam provincialibus et urbibus Africanis hac ratione concedimus ut ex his moenia publica restaurentur vel sarcientibus tecta substantia ministretur'.

well known that many cities in the less exposed parts of the African provinces had no fortifications till a very late date.[1] Possibly the incursions of nomads from the desert, which became serious in 363, were already threatening. About the same time as the date of this law, Fl. Archontius Nilus, governor of Tripolitania between 355 and 361, was engaged in military operations and the reconstruction of defences in his province.[2]

Shortly after this, Julian became emperor and introduced some further alleviations. By far the most important was the restoration to the cities of all their revenues and property.[3] No specific conditions were attached to this, but clearly the *curiales* were now freed—if the cities' property were large enough—from having to use their own resources to carry out such typical municipal responsibilities as fortification (already mentioned) and the maintenance of roads and public buildings. He further ordered that no burdens other than those already existing should be laid upon the *curiales* without his consent.[4] It seems also that the tax in gold and silver (*lustralis collatio*), which properly was paid by members of the mercantile corporations, had been exacted from *curiales*; they were now exempt from this, unless they engaged in trade.[5] Lastly, as well as the return of the Christian clergy to the *curiae*,[6] wealthy persons born in other cities were to be called to the *curia* of their place of residence.[7]

With the restoration of civic property, the position of the *curiales* was somewhat improved. There was thus a reason, beyond enthusiasm for Julian as a pagan emperor, for the renewal of rebuilding and the enthusiastic dedications in the African cities. However, the treasury was presumably unable to face this considerable loss of revenue; by 374, two thirds of the money was going to the treasury, one third being allowed to the cities for their buildings.[8] Such was the division of the income from city property at least until the end of the fourth century.[9]

The chief burden by which the *curiales* were oppressed was undoubtedly that of responsibility for the collection of taxes. The amount

---

[1] E.g. Carthage had none till 425. [2] C 11031 and *AE* (1895), 18.

[3] *Cod. Theod.* x. 3. 1; Amm. Marc. xxv. 4. 15, 'vectigalia civitatibus restituta cum fundis'. [4] *Cod. Theod.* xi. 16. 10.

[5] *Cod. Theod.* xii. 1. 50. These three laws of Julian, though under different titles in the Code, are parts of one law dealing with the position of the *curiales*, and dated 13 March 362. See also Ensslin, *Klio* xviii (1923), 132 ff.

[6] See above, p. 46. [7] *Cod. Theod.* xii. 1. 52.

[8] *Cod. Theod.* xv. 1. 18, iv. 13. 7. [9] *Cod. Theod.* xv. 1. 32, 33.

of revenue in money and in kind to be collected from each province was fixed by the praetorian prefect each year. In the provinces the amount due from each area was decided by accountants in the governor's staff. The actual collection was in the hands of *susceptores* chosen from the *curiales*. Any deficit in the amount due had to be made good, technically by the person who had proposed the *susceptor* who had failed,[1] but in fact probably by the whole *curia*. Obviously, since the amount of tax due was fixed according to the needs of the moment and with little regard for local conditions at any given time, every bad season or period of public disorder bore heavily on the *curiales*. This side of the case has always been the one most noted; but in the execution of their burdens, the *curiales* were not scrupulous, and the ultimate pressure was, as always, upon the peasant.[2] However, it can certainly be said that the removal of the burden of tax-collecting was the only thing which could save the curial class.

This was attempted by Valentinian and Valens. They ordered that the *susceptores* should in future be taken not from the *curiales* but from the officials (except the Palatine service).[3] As a natural development, the *praepositi horreorum*, who had charge of the warehouses in which taxes in kind were collected, were also taken from among the *officiales*.[4] *Exactores*, chosen from the wealthiest and hence most powerful *curiales*,[5] had had the task of applying pressure to persistently evasive tax-payers. It is probable that this duty also was now transferred to the *officiales*.[6]

It is permissible to agree with a recent historian of the fourth century,[7] that the *officiales* 'opposaient une résistance héroïque'. On the other hand Piganiol's conclusion that the reforms did not apply in Africa[8] seems erroneous. The law quoted by him to support this is addressed to Dracontius, vicar of Africa, and dated 365 or 368.[9] It states that a former law[10] had ordered that the *susceptores specierum* in the Illyrian provinces were to be chosen from the *officiales* because they were more

---

[1] *Cod. Theod.* XII. 6. 1.

[2] Salvian, *de Gub. Dei*, v. 18, 'ubi non quot fuerint curiales tot tyranni sunt'.

[3] *Cod. Theod.* VIII. 3. 1 (364), XII. 6. 6 (365).   [4] *Cod. Theod.* XII. 6. 5 (365).

[5] Two *exactores* appear among the *flamines perpetui* in the Album of Thamugadi.

[6] *Cod. Theod.* X. 24. 1 (365 or 373) implies this by numbering *exactores* with other persons known to be *officiales*.

[7] Piganiol, *L'Empire chrétien*, 172.

[8] Piganiol, *ibid.*   [9] *Cod. Theod.* XII. 6. 9.

[10] Presumably *Cod. Theod.* XII. 6. 7 (365).

suitable for the purpose, both in efficiency and honesty,[1] than the *curiales*. Dracontius is directed that in Africa the *susceptores specierum annonariarum* are to be taken from the *curiae* as before, since they are more easily held responsible for deficits.

It is, however, clear that the persons mentioned here are the collectors of the *species annonariae*. This was only a part, and indeed a small part, of the contribution in kind which had to be made by the African provinces largely to feed the city of Rome.[2] No other kind of tax is mentioned in the law. It is further most unlikely that the *officiales* were stronger and the *curiales* weaker in Africa than in the Illyrian provinces which were now under increasing pressure from the barbarians. Though some of the credit must doubtless go to official direction, some change for the better in the position of the *curiales* is required to explain the efforts made in rebuilding the African cities at this time, and the laws removing the burden of tax collection meet this requirement. The reimposition of the duty to collect the *species annonariae* would not detract much from the benefits conferred by the other reliefs.

The resistance of the *officiales* was, however, continuous and ultimately successful. At the very beginning, exemption was given to *officiales* in the Palatine service and on the staffs of the *magistri equitum* and *magistri peditum*.[3] In 383 came a law which presaged a return to the old system and which is most revealing about the social conditions of the time.[4] The *officiales* were made responsible for the collection of taxes from the *potentiores possessores*, *curiales* from their fellow members, and the *defensor civitatis* from the plebeians. In the first place, this shows the power of the wealthy landowners, who could only be compelled to pay their taxes by the *officiales*, who had, of course, the power of the governor and vicar behind them. Again, the plebeians were so oppressed first by the *curiales* and afterwards by the *officiales* that a special appointment, the *defensor civitatis*, was made to protect them. By 386, the burden was again resting entirely on the shoulders of the *curiales*.[5] It is from this date that the attempts to escape from the *curiae* even into a socially lower grade become more frequent, and, in Africa, the rebuilding which had been stimulated by Valentinian's reform comes to a rapid end.

---

[1] 're et fide'.   [2] See below, p. 59.   [3] *Cod. Theod.* XII. 6. 6 (365).
[4] *Cod. Theod.* XI. 7. 12.   [5] *Cod. Theod.* XII. 6. 20.

CHAPTER V

THE COUNTRY

IT is certain that with the exception of a few coastal cities like Carthage, Utica, and Hadrumetum, African towns were basically agricultural settlements in which a majority of the population gained their living from, and probably actually worked on, the land.[1] They were not primarily the residences of imperial officials, traders, and landowners. There seems to be little difference in this respect between the closely settled area in northern Tunisia, especially in the valley of the Bagradas, and the high plateaux of Algeria, though the date and origin of the settlement of the two areas were different, as was also the predominant crop. It is in these two areas that we see most clearly the characteristic of urban life in Africa in the large number of small but flourishing towns spread over considerable areas instead of a few cities of large size and little else but tribal agglomerations and hamlets as in the northern provinces of the Empire. This phenomenon bears witness to the intensity of the cultivation in the fertile areas and the consequent large population. The Carthaginians had started settled life in Tunisia, but in the high plains even in Tiberius' day there were no towns, and there is every indication that the native population was small.[2] Despite the emptiness of the land, the vast distances in Africa and the unsettled mountainous regions made for a lack of complete security and this is the most likely reason for the concentration of the greater part of the population in the towns. It seems probable that in these regions many even of the labourers lived in the towns during the winter and spent the summers in temporary dwellings in the fields, as is the custom today in several parts of the Mediterranean.

The northern part of Tunisia, the earliest area of Roman settlement which took over the civilizing work of the Carthaginians, was *par excellence* the area of wheat-growing, and it was here that there was the greatest concentration of towns and imperial estates. Next in importance as a cereal-producing area[3] was a narrow stretch of land extending

[1] See specially Sherwin-White, 'Geographical factors in Roman Algeria', *JRS* xxiv (1944), 8–10.   [2] Tac. *Ann.* II. 52. 3.
[3] Tenney Frank, *Economic Survey of Ancient Rome*, IV, 41.

from Veneria Sicca in the east to beyond Sitifis in the west. At its widest it extended only as far north as Calama and in the south to Madauros. To the north of it the forest-covered mountains precluded cultivation, while to the south the high plateaux stretching to the foot of the Aures range seem to have been more suitable for olives. Within it were the upper reaches of the Bagradas river, and the considerable towns of Bulla Regia, Naragarra and Thubursicu Numidarum as well as those just mentioned; further west were the chief towns of Numidia, Cirta, Milev and Cuicul, and the closely settled area round Sitifis. The exports from this long strip of territory were probably carried through Hippo Regius and Rusicade. The road Lambaesis–Cirta–Rusicade was difficult and doubtless had little significance in Mediterranean trade as a whole;[1] but that food for Rome passed through Rusicade—and hence by this road from central Numidia, Rusicade being otherwise isolated —is known from an inscription referring to the construction of *horrea* at the port *c*. 364–7 'ad securitatem populi Romani pariter ac provincialium'.[2]

After wheat, the most important African product was oil. This was a late-comer to North African agriculture; from the elder Pliny we learn that in the Flavian period olive cultivation was extremely slight.[3] The reason for this was undoubtedly the lack of complete security which alone would make the considerable investment needed profitable. In the second century A.D., however, olive-growing increased very rapidly and was encouraged by the emperors, in particular by Hadrian.[4] The areas in which it was most successful can be determined within reasonable limits by the number of oil presses which have been discovered. Unfortunately, few can be dated, but obviously by far the greater number must date from after the first century A.D., on the evidence of Pliny quoted above.

Tripolitania produced a considerable quantity of oil in the time of Julius Caesar[5] and Lepcis Magna paid a voluntary tribute of oil to Septimius Severus even though he had granted the *ius Italicum* to the city; this payment continued until the reign of Constantine.[6] The territory of Lepcis and the neighbouring cities of Sabrata and Oea was still productive of oil when it was ravaged several times between 363

[1] Sherwin-White, *loc. cit.*   [2] *C* 19852.
[3] Pliny, *N.H.* 15. 8.   [4] *C* 25943.
[5] Plutarch, *Caes.* 55.   [6] Aurel. Victor, *Caesares*, XLI. 19–20.

and 367 by the Austuriani.[1] The most considerable area in which olives were grown intensively was, however, the province of Byzacena, in particular a strip along the coast stretching from the region of Thysdrus to Thaenae and extending about thirty miles inland. It may be remarked that it is precisely in this area that French colonists have recently been most successful in growing olives.[2] Cultivation on a considerable scale took place all the way along the coast, and in some scattered inland districts such as Sufetula, Sufes and Maktar. An interesting inscription[3] from the coastal town of Uppena dating from the first half of the fifth century runs: 'P(ius) v(ir) Dion bixsit annos octogenta et instituit arbores quatuor milia.' The trees planted by this Christian landowner can only have been olives. This is, I believe, an almost unique recognition from the western provinces, at least from so late a date, of such a form of beneficial activity. We may compare an inscription, of the fourth century at the earliest, from the country near Hippo Regius which records the establishment of an estate with a well, baths and 'hortum omnibus pomis diversis institutum'.[4]

The second large area of olive cultivation extended from Theveste along the northern slope of the Aures mountains and the Bou Taleb range and also between the Aures and the Hodna. Particularly fertile in this area was the district bounded by Zarai, Nicivibus, and Diana Veteranorum.[5] This intensity of olive-growing in a region close to the un-romanized mountain ranges is an indication of the security provided by the *limes*. In the proconsular province, where the main crop was wheat, olive-growing on the less fertile parts of the imperial estates was encouraged by the emperors of the second century.[6]

The areas mentioned above are those in which the respective crops were so extensively grown as to leave little doubt that much of the produce was exported. In other less fertile areas of North Africa, farming was mainly for subsistence. Yet even in Mauretania Caesariensis there were areas in which wealthy Romans thought it worth while to have interests. Towards the end of the fourth century, the orator Symmachus had an estate there,[7] and several inscriptions record the construction of forts on the landowner's property[8]—a phenomenon

---

[1] Amm. Marc. xxviii. 6. 13 mentions the deliberate destruction of the olives and vines.
[2] Despois, *La Tunisie orientale, passim.*   [3] *ILT* 243.
[4] *ILAlg* 158.   [5] Gsell, *Atlas arch. Alg.* Map 16.
[6] *C* 25902 (Hr. Mettich), 25943 (Ain-el-Djemala).   [7] Symm. *Ep.* vii. 661.
[8] E.g. *C* 9725, 20816.

found all over the Empire in the third and fourth centuries because of the prevailing insecurity (though examples have yet to be recorded in Proconsularis and Byzacena).

It is difficult to estimate the level of agricultural production in the fourth century because of the almost complete lack of references to it. In general, however, it seems to have remained high. The devastations in Africa caused by civil wars and barbarian raids, though severe in some areas, were by no means as serious as in other parts of the western half of the Empire, especially Gaul. They appear to have caused no radical disturbance to the cultivation of the olive which, requiring the constant maintenance of the systems of water conservation, would have been the first to decline in times of serious unrest, even if the trees were not actually destroyed. In fact, the systems of conservation and irrigation which the Romans introduced survived even the Vandal and Moorish wars of the sixth century to surprise the Arabs in many places in the seventh.[1] The *Expositio totius mundi*, written about the middle of the fourth century, states that Africa exported oil to almost all parts of the world.[2] Further, along the high plains north of the Aures were a very large number of native villages of the Roman period, in addition to the actual Roman foundations. The evidence seems to show that this area was sparsely populated before the second century,[3] and the fact that few, if any, of these developed into *civitates*—though they may well have been as populous—would indicate that their growth was later than the great period of African town life which ended in 238. This increased population was doubtless paralleled by greater production. From the numerous references to the plight of Rome when there was any interruption in the supply of food from Africa, it is clear that its agricultural products were much in demand, and that a surplus must have continued.

The importance of Africa as a source of food for the city of Rome is attested as early as A.D. 68, when the governor Clodius Macer revolted against Nero[4] and famine was threatened at Rome. At the end of the second century, Septimius Severus was obliged to send a considerable force to Africa[5] to prevent Niger getting control there, and thus oppressing the people of Rome by cutting off supplies of corn. The disorders of the third century, not less in Italy than in other provinces,

---

[1] E.g. references in Gsell, *Atlas arch. Alg.* s.v. Badias.
[2] Expositio, 61, in *Geographici Latini Minores*, ed. Riese.
[3] Above, p. 55.   [4] Tac. *Hist.* I. 73.   [5] SHA, *Vita Sev.* 8.

only increased this dependence. The revolt of Domitius Alexander against Maxentius in 308–11 is explicitly stated to have caused a shortage in Rome.[1]

The word *annona*, more fully *annona civica*, was used both for the food itself and for the whole system of supply.[2] Before the foundation of Constantinople, the burden of supplying Rome had been shared between Africa and Egypt. Subsequently, however, the surplus from Egypt had to supply the new capital, and Rome became dependent on Africa alone.[3] In view of the decline of Italian agriculture and the frequent devastation by the Germans of alternative sources in Gaul, the importance of the African provinces in the economy of the western half of the Empire naturally increased. From the middle of the fourth century onwards we have a succession of notices of food shortages in Rome as a result of failure in Africa, and various special measures taken by the emperors to defend the province. In 361, Constantius, hearing of the elevation of Julian in Gaul, sent the *notarius* Gaudentius into Africa, 'a province most advantageous to the emperors at all periods', to forestall his rival.[4] But when we arrive at the last two decades of the fourth century, a period covered by the correspondence of Symmachus, the utter dependence of Rome and probably most of the large cities of North Italy on African supplies becomes manifest. In 383, there was famine[5] in the southern half of the Empire, both east and west, much aggravated 'cum provinciis Africis nec ad victum tenuem frugum tritura responderit, et adportata ex aliis terris semina vicinus annus expectet'.[6] Symmachus urged the emperors in 384/5 to give stricter orders to the governors of the African provinces about the despatch of the *annona*, since both wheat and oil were scarce in the city.[7] Five years later 'paene cessante Africa, fames in limine erat'.[8] In 395 a delay in the arrival of the corn ships brought further alarm,[9] and a shortage in 396 is implied in a letter by the orator to Florentinus in 397 ('Absit ut praesens annus imitetur fortunam superiorum').[10] These delays were due to the actions of Gildo, count of Africa, who finally withdrew his allegiance

---

[1] Eumen. *Paneg.* IV. 9.
[2] Cagnat, 'L'Annona d'Afrique', in *Mémoires de l'Académie des inscriptions et belles lettres* (1916).
[3] Claud. *de Bell. Gild.* 52 ff.   [4] Amm. Marc. XXI. 7. 2; see also XXVI. 4. 5.
[5] Ambr. *Ep.* I. 18. 21.   [6] Symm. *Ep.* IV. 74.
[7] Symm. *Ep.* X. 18. 35.   [8] Symm. *Ep.* III. 55.
[9] Symm. *Ep.* VII. 68.   [10] Symm. *Ep.* IV. 54.

from Honorius and gave it to the more distant emperor of the East, Arcadius. This was in the autumn of 397, and thus there was no shipment in the following summer. The defeat of Gildo by the forces sent by Honorius in 398 brought with it hopes of a better position with the arrival of captured supplies,[1] but the next year there was a further shortage. In one of his latest letters (402), however, Symmachus congratulates the proconsul of Africa for promising 'largas rei annonariae copias'.[2] In 409 Attalus was recognized at Rome as Western emperor on the orders of Alaric. Heraclian, the *comes Africae*, wishing to preserve the province for Honorius, repulsed an attempt by the usurper on Africa, and prevented supplies leaving, with the usual consequences for Rome.[3] When Heraclian himself revolted against Honorius, he again stopped the *annona* (413).[4] These numerous references, in the correspondence of Symmachus especially, show the importance attached to the regular arrival of the *annona*, and the fears aroused in Rome at the slightest delay.[5] The organization and maintenance of this vital service were most important to the emperors of the fourth century. It was also the greatest burden the African provinces had to bear. No area escaped some exaction, for besides wheat, large quantities of oil were sent to Rome,[6] and to a lesser degree various other commodities such as wine, fat, and fruit included in the term *species annonariae*.[7]

We are well informed about the method of collection in the fourth century. Whether the land concerned belonged to the state, the cities, or private persons, those responsible for paying their portion had to deliver it at fixed intervals (three times a year) at the municipal granaries (*horrea*).[8] It was then the responsibility of the municipalities to transport the supplies to centres under the control of the *fiscus* (*horrea fiscalia*), administered by *praepositi horreorum*.[9]

The ultimate authorities over these two stages (*exactio* or *conlatio*, and *transmissio*) were the proconsul in his province, and the vicar in the other provinces.[10] Responsible for the centralization and dispatch

---

[1] Symm. *Ep.* VII. 38.   [2] Symm. *Ep.* V. 94.
[3] Zosim. VI. 7.   [4] Orosius, VII. 42. 12.
[5] Compare the similar fears in Constantinople at delays in supplies from Egypt shown, for example, by the circumstances of the execution of Sopater in 331 (Eunap. *Vit. Sophist.* 462), and the accusations brought against Athanasius in 335 (*Apol. c. Arianos*, 9).
[6] *Cod. Theod.* XIV. 15. 3.   [7] *Cod. Theod.* XII. 6. 15.
[8] *Cod. Theod.* XI .1. 2.   [9] *Cod. Theod.* VII. 4.
[10] *Cod. Theod.* I. 15. 14 (395). From this date the vicar was responsible in Africa Proconsularis also.

(*pervectio*) to Rome was the *vir clarissimus praefectus annonae Africae*, who was subordinate directly to the praetorian prefect, and appears for the first time at the beginning of the fourth century.[1] The chief assistants of the *praefectus annonae* were the *navicularii*. These were the merchants who transported, or organized, the transport of the *annona*. They were already formed into corporations in the early days of the Empire, but at that time were merely traders and not specifically concerned with the transport of the *annona* unless they had contracted to do so. By the time of Septimius Severus, those who did undertake the *annona* were given exemption from the municipal burdens they should, by virtue of wealth or birth, have carried out in their home towns. This was justified on the grounds that the supply of food to Rome was in effect a *munus publicum*, and it was thus reasonable to exempt from other charges those who had undertaken it.[2] It was not yet compulsory for the *navicularii* of Africa to undertake the burden; but as soon as immunity from municipal burdens was considered as attached to the corporation and the corporation as invested with a public duty, it appeared as an official institution for carrying out a public service.[3]

The disorders of the third century fell very hard on the merchants as on the middle class as a whole. At the same time the requirements of the state continually increased. It was thus inevitable that the emperors should use compulsion to fill the gaps caused by failures and to maintain the increased service. The *navicularii* throughout the Empire were affected. There was now no freedom for the individual or for his corporation. The service became a *functio*; it involved the *navicularius* in the confiscation of his property in case of loss, shipwreck or default;[4] and the heir of a *navicularius* had to fulfil the burden if he accepted the legacy. It was for this reason that St Augustine refused to accept a legacy from a *navicularius* to his church. The privileges given in return were, for the *navicularii* of Africa, summed up in the phrase 'privilegia Africana'.[5] Of these, the chief was the complete exemption from municipal charges[6] which they had originally been given at the end of the second century. They were also freed from the

---

[1] *Cod. Theod.* XI. 30. 4 (315). The office could, of course, have been in existence some time before this.
[2] *Dig.* L. 6. 3 and 5.
[3] Waltzing, *Étude historique sur les corporations professionnelles chez les Romains*, II, 49 ff.
[4] *Cod. Theod.* XIII. 5. 3, 5 etc.   [5] *Cod. Theod.* XIII. 5. 14.
[6] *Cod. Theod.* XIII. 5. 5 (326).

port charges on merchandise which they carried for their own trade. Lastly the equestrian status exempted them from corporal punishments.

The supply of corn to Rome by Africa was technically called the *annona civica*. In common with all other provinces, however, she had to provide supplies for the local garrison and for the payment or part payment in kind of the officials. The *annona militaris*, as this exaction was termed, though burdensome, cannot have formed more than a small proportion of the whole *annona*. It was the excessive demands made by armies when campaigning which caused hardship. Two instances from Africa reveal this clearly. The count Romanus refused to assist the cities of Tripolitania to drive out the barbarians who had attacked their territory unless they handed over the enormous amount of 4000 camels together with supplies. The cities, after their losses through devastation, were quite unable to do this, and suffered accordingly.[1] On the other hand, the behaviour of Theodosius, the father of the emperor, during his campaign against the revolt of Firmus in Mauretania, in refusing to exact supplies from the provincials gained him the astonished gratitude of the landowners.[2]

The wealth of Africa being very largely in agriculture, the distribution of landed property among various kinds of owner was of great political and social importance. The largest landowner in Africa was undoubtedly the emperor. The process by which much of the most fertile land came into his possession doubtless began early, and was accelerated by Nero, as we learn from a well-known passage in Pliny.[3] This was at first mostly in the proconsular province, but there were also imperial estates in Numidia and Mauretania in the reign of Hadrian.[4] Throughout the succeeding two centuries the process continued, by purchase, bequest or confiscation.[5] At the end of the fourth century a notable acquisition was the property of Gildo which was so extensive that a special officer, the *comes Gildoniaci patrimonii*, was created to supervise it.[6] The African provinces were not unique in this great expansion of the wealth of the emperor, but there is no doubt that owing to their fertility and security they attracted imperial attention more than

---

[1] Amm. Marc. XXVIII. 6. 6.   [2] Amm. Marc. XXVIII. 5. 10.

[3] Pliny, *N.H.* 18. 35; 'sex domini semissem Africae possidebant cum interfecit eos Nero'.

[4] *C* 8810–12.

[5] See Kornemann, *P-W*, Suppl. IV, 249 ff., for the concentration of imperial estates in Africa.   [6] *Notit. Occ.* XII.

most others. In Africa there was not only a *rationalis rei privatae* subordinate, like the *rationales* of other dioceses, to the *comes rerum privatarum*, but a *procurator rei privatae per Mauretaniam Sitifensem*.[1] This indicates the survival of a large concentration of imperial property north of the Bou Taleb mountains, some fifty miles long from east to west and about half that width, which had existed for some two centuries.[2] Also unique in the list of administrators of imperial property given in the *Notitia Dignitatum* is the *rationalis rei privatae fundorum domus divinae per Africam*. The *fundi domus divinae* seem to have been divided from the *res privata* in the second half of the fourth century and the income derived from them devoted to the maintenance of the court. This distinction appeared later in parts of the Eastern Empire in particular.[3]

Unfortunately, too few of the actual estates have been identified to permit a clear picture of their distribution to be given. Doubtless the wealth of Gildo was almost entirely in Mauretania. If the imperial estates known from the second century continued in the hands of the emperor,[4] however, there can be little doubt that the most considerable number were in Africa Proconsularis. This after all is what would logically be expected, when we consider the greater fertility and security of that province.

A law dated 422 not only confirms this, but gives exact figures—a great rarity in the economic history of the ancient world—for the imperial estates in both Africa Proconsularis and Byzacena.[5] The figures given are:

Proconsularis	Land under cultivation	9002	centuries
	Land uncultivated	5700	,,
	Total[6]	14702	,,
Byzacena	Land under cultivation	7460	,,
	Land uncultivated	7615	,,
	Total[7]	15075	,,

[1] *Notit. Occ.* XII.
[2] The boundaries are indicated by *C* 8810–12 and 20487.
[3] *Notit. Occ.* XII; Kornemann, *loc. cit.* 262.
[4] *C* 25902, 25943, 10570, the well-known inscriptions of Hr. Mettich, Ain-el-Djemala, and Souk-el-Khmis. See also J. van Nostrand, *The Imperial Domains of Africa Proconsularis*.
[5] *Cod. Theod.* XI. 28. 13. Commentary by Barthel, *Bonner Jahrbücher* (1911), 49 ff.
[6] About 2950 square miles.   [7] About 3000 square miles.

The totals represent one-fifth of the area of Proconsularis and one-seventh of that of Byzacena. This is obviously very considerable, particularly when we consider the amount of unproductive land in Byzacena, much of which was probably left in the hands of natives, and the density of the towns, each with its surrounding territory, in Proconsularis. The amount of uncultivated land within the imperial estates is also not excessive;[1] in much of the interior of Byzacena, the land was hard and needed careful irrigation which might omit large parts of some estates. In Proconsularis, apart from wooded areas, land was given over to pasture for stock-breeding;[2] both of these would be considered uncultivated. These figures thus show a continued, extensive exploitation.

Africa had early been notorious as a land of huge estates in the hands of private persons.[3] This continued to be the case despite confiscations by the emperors and the disorders of the third century. When we come to the fourth century, we find numerous references in St Augustine's letters to wealthy landowners. Some lived in Africa,[4] while others were absentees.[5] Symmachus, whose fortune was moderate[6] compared with that of a Probus or an Ausonius, possessed an estate in Mauretania.[7] The powerful family of the Ceionii had an estate near Tubernuc in a very fertile part of the proconsular province.[8] St Melania, undoubtedly one of the wealthiest of all the subjects of the emperor at the beginning of the fifth century, had estates in Proconsularis, Numidia and Mauretania;[9] one, near Thagaste in Proconsularis, was itself larger than the territory of that city,[10] with its own baths and workers in gold, silver and bronze. Very probably most estates of this order were self-supporting. Mosaics of the period such as that from the villa of the landowner Julius of Carthage, though not as numerous as those of the second and

[1] Ausonius, *Idyll*, III. 21, mentions an estate in Gaul which he considers to be of moderate size, of about 650 acres. Only one-third of this was cultivated, the remainder being woodland. There is nothing to show he thought this a high proportion of uncultivated land. See also Barthel, *loc. cit.* 50, and Rostovtzeff, *op. cit.* 591.

[2] Gauckler, *Inventaire des mosaiques*, III. 260, 262, 263.

[3] Pliny, *N.H.* 18. 35.

[4] Aug. *Epp.* 56, 89. (See also *Epp.* 29. 2, 35. 2, 105. 3, for estates near Hippo Regius; *de Civitat. Dei*, XXII. 8, near Carthage.)

[5] Aug. *Ep.* 58.

[6] Olympiodorus in Photius, *Bibl.* LXXX (Migne, *PG* CIII, 278).

[7] Symm. *Ep.* VII. 66.   [8] *C* 25990.

[9] *Vita S. Mel.* 10 in *Analect. Boll.* VIII (1889), 16 ff.

[10] *Vita S. Mel.* 21; cf. Frontin. *de Controv. agr.* 53 for earlier estates of this size in Africa.

early third centuries, give an idea of the continued prosperity and luxury of the upper class.[1]

The total amount of land owned by the *curiales* must also have been considerable. Mention has already been made of the fact that there were clearly great differences of wealth in each city. Although all members of the *curiae* were liable to similar burdens, it is clear that only the wealthiest would in fact be elected to offices entailing great expense. In the law[2] laying down penalties for adherence to Donatism after its final condemnation, *sacerdotales* rank above *principales* (the title given to a certain number, usually ten, of the wealthiest *curiales*)[3] and are equal with *viri clarissimi*. They were thus among the most considerable men in the province. But in general, the landed property of a *curialis* was a security which was forfeit if he deserted his position in society. His rights of alienation were consequently severely limited by a series of laws.[4] Land was in fact the chief source of wealth for the African *curiales*, just as it had been in the second century.[5]

The changes in ownership of lands belonging to the municipalities themselves are more fully discussed elsewhere.[6] Briefly, they were appropriated to the fiscus by Constantine, but restored partially by Constantius and completely by Julian; from the time of Valentinian, two thirds of the revenue went to the treasury, one third to the cities. Some cities had jurisdiction over large areas,[7] and it is probable that their property was correspondingly extensive. Further large areas, mostly of inferior or mountainous lands, were occupied by Moorish tribes. The two churches of Africa likewise became wealthy in landed property. The Donatist bishop of Calama was able to purchase an estate on which lived over eighty *coloni*,[8] or serfs; doubtless many Catholic churches became even wealthier through the gifts and legacies of wealthy members.[9] Augustine tells us that the property of the

---

[1] *BAC* (1921), 95 ff. (mosaic of Julius at Carthage); Gauckler, *op. cit.* II, 940.

[2] *Cod. Theod.* XVI. 5. 52 (412).

[3] Their fine is four times that of the ordinary *curialis*. In the later scale of fines, *Cod. Theod.* XVI. 5. 54 (414), they are called *decem primi curiales*.

[4] E.g *Cod. Theod.* XII. 3 (386) requires the *curialis* to obtain the governor's permission before selling his property.

[5] Rostovtzeff, *op. cit.* 292.

[6] Above, pp. 51 ff.

[7] E.g. Thugga in Proconsularis and Cirta in Numidia.

[8] Aug. *contra Litt. Pet.* II. 83. 184 and *Ep.* 66 (402).

[9] St Melania gave her estate near Thagaste to the Church; *Vita*, 21.

Church of Hippo Regius was twenty times as large as the estate (admittedly small) which he had inherited from his father.[1]

This completes the survey of landownership in Africa; we have now to consider the persons—the great majority of the population—who worked the land. It can be said that during the fourth century, their position gradually deteriorated until in places it came to resemble that form of tenancy known to the European Middle Ages as serfdom.[2] In general terms, the *coloni* of the fourth century were tenants who paid as rent a varying proportion of the produce of the land they farmed and in many cases worked a certain number of days each year on that part of the estate which was farmed by the landowner himself or his representative. During the fourth century it became a crime for the *colonus* to leave his estate and the position became hereditary;[3] land-owners were forbidden to sell land without the *coloni* who cultivated it.[4] Later, a similar restraint was put upon the sale of rural slaves (*rustici servi*)[5]—a clear indication that the rural slave at this time was in fact a tenant farmer, and thus in a better position than his forerunners of the early Empire. These laws were not made in the interests of the land-owners, but to prevent the land going out of cultivation[6] with consequent loss to the treasury. They did ultimately benefit the landowners, who wished to have as many *coloni* as possible. Pressure on the lower classes in the country to become *coloni* was in fact almost irresistible. Free small-holders might voluntarily seek the protection of a landowner in time of trouble, or accept his financial help at the price of becoming his *colonus*.[7] In many cases violence was used by powerful lords.[8] Free tenants were easily reduced by such pressure even before the laws tied them to the soil. Finally the rural slaves advanced in status because their replacement was becoming increasingly difficult and more profit could be made from them as *coloni* than as mere agricultural workers.

[1] Aug. *Ep.* 126. 7.

[2] See Rostovtzeff, *Studien zur Geschichte des römischen Kolonats*; also Seeck *P-W* IV, 497 ff.

[3] *Cod. Theod.* V. 17. 1; but see Stein, *op. cit.* 22, for a third century date.

[4] *Cod. Just.* XI. 48. 2 (357).

[5] *Cod. Just.* XI. 48. 7 (between 367 and 376).

[6] Often unsuccessfully. In 395, in Campania alone, over half a million *jugera* are recorded as having gone out of cultivation (*Cod. Theod.* XI. 28. 2).

[7] Salvian, *de Gub. Dei*, v. 39–44. These were the most frequent means by which free peasants became *coloni*.

[8] *Cod. Theod.* III. 1. 9 (415); 'transactiones quae per potentiam extortae sunt, praecipimus infirmari'.

Those who were still used in the latter manner worked on the part of the estate farmed by the lord himself, with the occasional help of the *coloni*. There were finally large numbers of broken men who had deserted their farms from poverty or oppression by officials, and *curiales* who found their burdens too great, who were protected by the powerful despite the severe laws against such patronage.[1] It is indeed probable that in this, as in other types of social deterioration, the position in Africa was not so bad as in other provinces. The *circumcelliones* were free agricultural labourers,[2] and the type of land tenure known as the Mancian colonate, which implied free peasant farmers, survived till Vandal times.[3] However, as the position of nearly all the country folk worsened, that of the landowners became more powerful. The *potentes*, as they came to be called, were able to protect their less powerful clients from the pressure, not necessarily illegal, of officers of the fiscus, and corrupt the judiciary.[4] The same applies to the *procuratores* and *conductores*, the managers of estates of absentee landlords and of the *res privata*.[5] Their direct power over their *coloni* was in practice almost absolute. Thus in Africa, the Donatist serfs of the Catholic Pammachius[6] and the Catholic serfs of Crispinus, Donatist bishop of Calama,[7] were forcibly converted to the religion of their masters. The latter case is the more remarkable when we consider that Crispinus was farming a piece of imperial property, and that frequent laws against Donatism had been made during the previous thirty years. Confident of the orthodoxy of the landlords, or despairing of the conduct of the officials, in 412 Honorius required the former to redeem their *coloni* from Donatism.[8] A further law on the same matter two years later gave still greater power and responsibility to the *conductores* and landlords.[9] 'If the *conductores* of our [i.e. imperial] estates permit Donatism to continue, they are to be fined a year's salary..., if *conductores* of private estates allow Donatists to meet on the estates

---

[1] *Cod. Theod.* XII. 1. 179 (415). See also the whole title 'de patrociniis vicorum', *Cod. Theod.* XI. 24, and F. de Zulueta, *Patronage in the Later Empire.*

[2] Below, pp. 84 ff.　　[3] Albertini, *Journal des Savants* (1930), 23–30.

[4] *Cod. Theod.* XI. 24. 4 (399); even *curiales* were guilty of this; *Cod. Theod.* I. 16. 13 (377).

[5] *Cod. Theod.* I. 16. 14 (408).　　[6] Aug. *Ep.* 58.

[7] Aug. *contra Litt. Pet.* II. 83. 184.

[8] *Cod. Theod.* XVI. 5. 52; 'servos dominorum admonitio vel colonos verberum crebrior ictus a prava religione revocabit'.

[9] *Cod. Theod.* XVI. 5. 54.

they are to be brought to the notice of their employers, who if they wish to escape the penalties themselves must correct the erring and employ *conductores* who will obey the laws.'

Such constitutions show how far in certain matters the state was prepared to allow the *potentes* personal power over their dependants. In general, however, their activity is unlikely to have been as black as has been painted. The laws for the suppression of Donatism are exceptional in their grant to the landowners of what amounted to private justice. It is unrealistic to deduce from the admittedly numerous laws dealing with all kinds of abuses of power by the *potentes* that such behaviour was the general rule. It may further be noted that as in the case of the flight of *curiales* to lower positions in society these laws only became frequent at the end of the century. Some landlords, even in enlightened self-interest, were good. The serfs of St Melania, who had worked for the same family for three generations, called their owners their friends and created a disturbance when it was thought they were to be disposed of outside the family.[1] Finally, even if the position of a *colonus* was hard and humiliating, the protection of a powerful landlord and his fortified villa was some compensation in the late fourth century and after. Such self-sufficient units of society were more a symptom than a cause of the decline of the Empire; when it finally disintegrated they survived—in other western provinces, if not in Africa. There the influx of Moors and Arabs was so large that civilization was swept entirely away.

[1] *Vita S. Mel.* 10. Many followed Melania to Africa and entered the convents founded by her.

CHAPTER VI

THE MOORS AND THE ROMANS

THERE can be no doubt that in the fourth century the racial composition of the people of North Africa was similar to what it had been two hundred years before when the Berber and Punic natives formed by far the largest part of the population.[1] There was no large immigration from Italy after the beginning of the Empire, and towards the middle of the second century, the Third Legion which garrisoned Africa was largely recruited on the spot. It has been demonstrated that even in the cities of the proconsular provinces, where Roman influence was undoubtedly strongest, many names found on inscriptions which are apparently Roman are in fact translations of native names;[2] while the use of the latter, though on a diminishing scale, continued throughout the period of the Empire. Native preponderance in Numidia and Mauretania, where the cities were fewer in number, and the proportion of Italian immigrants smaller, must have been even greater. We should not, however, overemphasize this numerical inferiority. The attraction of Roman civilization was very strong, particularly among the native aristocracy whether tribal or city-dwelling, and these people became indistinguishable from the descendants of Italian immigrants. Examples of the advance of such families may be found in the Memmii of Gigthis, the first of whom has the name of his obscure tribe recorded on an inscription,[3] and the Gabinii of Thugga.[4] The process continued into the fourth century; in 320, a Christian of Cirta who called himself 'professor Romanarum litterarum, grammaticus Latinus', was the son of a *decurio* of Cirta, the grandson of a soldier in the *comitatus* who was of Moorish blood.[5] Doubtless every town-dweller in the fourth century had some native

---

[1] *Economic Survey of Ancient Rome*, ed. T. Frank, IV, 106. See also Rostovtzeff, *Social and Economic History of the Roman Empire*, 291–3.

[2] Toutain, *Les Cités romaines de la Tunisie*, 167–96.

[3] *C* 22729; 'L. Memmio L. f. Quir. Pacato fl. perp. divi Traiani Chinithio in quinque decurias a divo Hadriano adlecto Chinithi ob merita...et pietatem qua nationi suae praestat...posuerunt'. See also *C* 22741, 22718, 22719; Rostovtzeff, *op. cit.* 292.

[4] *ILT* 1511–13, 1391; *C* 26517; T. R. S. Broughton, *op. cit.* 59, note 83 (but read A.D. 48 for 48 B.C.).

[5] Appendix I to Optatus, *CSEL* XXVI, 185.

blood in his veins, but in Proconsularis at least, where the towns were so numerous, these persons must have formed as romanized a population as could be found outside Italy.

In Numidia and Mauretania, as has been said, the position was different. There were indeed areas of some degree of romanization, such as the north-western plains of the Aures where settlements of veterans had been frequent in the second century. But over much of the area of these provinces the native population can only have been influenced by Roman civilization through the presence of military detachments and the introduction by landowners of efficient irrigation and a settled agricultural life. There were also the large areas of mountain ranges in which Moorish tribes lived in virtual independence. It has in fact been maintained[1] that the Romans withdrew from much of Mauretania Caesariensis, including part of the un-romanized region, towards the end of the third century. The reason put forward for this move was the decision of Diocletian at the outset of his reign to evacuate the city of Volubilis in Mauretania Tingitana and withdraw the southern boundary of that province to the line of the Oued Loukkos and the Oued Laon, which enclosed no more than the peninsula of Tangier opposite Gibraltar, an area only one-tenth of that of the original province. Since this disrupted the lateral communications supposed to exist between Mauretania Tingitana and Mauretania Caesariensis the whole of Mauretania Caesariensis west of the mouth of the Oued Chelif was evacuated. Thus the western boundary of Roman North Africa would have been the line of Oued Hammam.

The withdrawal in Mauretania Tingitana had certainly taken place by the end of the fourth century; this can be gathered from the account of the dispositions of the *limitanei* in the province given in the *Notitia Dignitatum*.[2] The evidence for its having taken place a century earlier in the reign of Diocletian is almost conclusive. The latest inscription from Volubilis implying Roman rule is from 283 to 284,[3] and the coinage comes to an abrupt end there at the same date.[4] On the other hand, the evidence presented for a withdrawal in Mauretania Caesariensis is not convincing. The chief point is the lack of milestones which

---

[1] Carcopino, *Le Maroc antique*, 231 ff.   [2] *Occ.* XXIV.
[3] *ILA* 618, erasure of the name of Probus.
[4] Carcopino, *op. cit.* 248. The total number of coins found, nearly 3000, makes this significant.

are later than the reign of Carus (283). But an inscription from Albulae,[1] dating from 299, records the restoration of a temple and names a *curator ac dispunctor, duoviri* and *aediles*. Later still is one from Numerus Syrorum,[2] dated between 344 and 348 which reads 'pro salute atq(ue) incolumitate DD.NN. impp.Constanti et Constans Augg. Muru et porta nova et turres a solo Statulenius Felix disp(unctor) una cum primores dedicavit (anno) P(rovinciae) CCCV...(344–8)'. It is impossible (despite the Latinity) that these inscriptions could have been set up long after the end of Roman rule. Neither did the cutting of the road (if it existed) between Mauretania Caesariensis and Tingitana necessitate such a withdrawal in the former province; the Oued Mouloucha had formerly been the boundary of the two provinces, and there is no reason to believe that it did not form the western boundary of Caesariensis during much of the fourth century. The fact that this left a salient of barbarian territory between it and Tingitana was doubtless one of the reasons which made the attachment of the latter province to the diocese of Spain inevitable. It is further clear that the withdrawal from Volubilis was the result of pressure against the southern border of the province from a Moorish tribe, the Baquates, which had been increasing for half a century.[3] There is no indication of any threat of this kind in Mauretania Caesariensis.

The later history of this area is still more obscure. There are no more inscriptions which indicate the presence of the Roman administration; but only one[4] occurs in all the rest of the province about which there is no question. When we consider the number of Christian epitaphs dating from the fourth century and later which have been found in the west of the province it is perhaps noteworthy that among the numerous Mauretanian bishoprics mentioned in the acts of the Conference of Carthage (411) the most westerly is Aquae Sirenses, situated on the Oued Hammam. It is thus possible that at this date the area under Roman control stretched no further west. A similar conclusion is indicated by the lack of *limes* sector headquarters to the west of Columnata, itself well to the east of the Oued Hammam. Admittedly, there are six unidentified places mentioned in the sections of the *Notitia Dignitatum* concerned with the Mauretanian *limes*, but it is difficult to

---

[1] *C* 21665. [2] *AE* (1935), 86.

[3] Carcopino, *op. cit.* 267 ff.

[4] *C* 9547, p. 974 (Caesarea), between 379 and 383 or 408 and 423.

imagine that these controlled the huge area between Columnata and the Oued Moulouya, particularly as none of the towns there, most of which had been forts in the early Empire, are among them. It is tempting, but admittedly unprovable, to suppose that a withdrawal was made after the revolt of Firmus, with a closer watch being kept on some of the tribes instead of a weak defence against all.

The Vandals, on the other hand, passed through the region of Altava[1] in 429, and certainly controlled it in 484. At that date a conference was called to Carthage by Hunneric to decide between the Arian and Catholic faiths. Catholic bishops came from Altava, Pomaria, Numerus Syrorum, Albulae and other places from that district as yet unidentified.[2] The Moors living in the region must have been in a state of subjection for their bishops thus to risk martyrdom or exile, for the result of the conference was a foregone conclusion.[3]

A remarkable series of inscriptions dating from the fifth to the seventh century enable us to put a slightly higher estimate on the influence of Roman civilization on the Moors than has usually been done. Out of some seventy Christian inscriptions[4] dating between A.D. 450 and 651 from Mauretania Caesariensis, fifty are from the region west of the mouth of the Oued Chelif, most from Pomaria, Altava and Albulae. The inscriptions are in Latin not inferior in any way to that of contemporary examples found in the more romanized provinces. The persons mentioned, both men and women, have Latin names, usually two, as had long been the custom in much of Africa.[5] (Some earlier inscriptions of a similar type give the *tria nomina*.)[6] The usual formula gives the name of the deceased followed by the relatives who have made the tomb, usually called *domus aeternalis* or *aeterna*. In Africa this usage is confined to Mauretania, though examples occur in Italy.[7] The local usage is also conservative in that the formula D(is) M(anibus) S(acrum), which was originally pagan, and though Christianized had early dropped out of use in the rest of Africa, is almost the rule. Again, names of a specifically Christian nature, like Adeodatus or Deusdedit, which were very popular in the rest of Africa—and indeed throughout

---

[1] *AE* (1935), 85.
[2] E.g. Castra Severiana, *C* 9836. Victor de Vita, *Notitia Episcoporum*, *CSEL* VII, 128–31.　　　　　　　　　　　　　　　　　[3] Victor de Vita, II, 38 ff.
[4] Diehl, *ILCV* III, 270 ff.
[5] Cf. *C* 2403 and 17824, the Album of Thamugadi.
[6] E.g. *C* 9966, Numerus Syrorum (402).　　[7] Carcopino, *Rev. Phil.* LXII (1936), 106.

the west—do not occur. This conservatism is doubtless due to the isolation of these regions even when they were not independent. A typical example of these inscriptions is[1]

D M S
Nonnea Prima
vix(it) an(nos) LXXX
cui fili(us) fecit
dom(um) eternalem
An(no) (Provinciae) DXVIII (547)

A similar series of inscriptions has recently been found at Volubilis,[2] dating between 599 and 655, shortly before the Arab conquest. No Christian remains from Volubilis are earlier than these, but this does not mean they may not yet be discovered.[3] What is remarkable is that the inscriptions both of Volubilis and western Mauretania Caesariensis use the Roman provincial era of Mauretania for dating as late as three hundred years after the end of Roman rule. We may compare the dating of monuments in Burgundy from the consulships of Justinus (540) and Basilius (541) till the seventh century.[4]

It seems likely, therefore, that the growth of Christianity in these wilder parts of Mauretania, so far from being interrupted by the disappearance of Roman rule, at whatever date that took place, received new impetus. The Latin language continued to be used at least for religious purposes,[5] and men and women bore Latin names. This is particularly noticeable at Volubilis, where the inscriptions are centuries after the Roman withdrawal. It seems possible both from similarities in the inscriptions themselves, and the epitaph at Volubilis of a woman 'de Altava ko(o)ptativa' that there was contact between the two places, and that at some date the whole of the area west of the Chelif was controlled by the tribe of the Baquates with its capital at Volubilis, now Christian in faith and to some extent still under the spell of Roman civilization.[6]

---

[1] *C* 9939, Pomaria.

[2] Carcopino, *loc. cit.* 105 ff.

[3] *Passio Marcelli*, in *Analect. Boll.* XII (1923), 2603 ff., indicates Christians at Tingi during the reign of Diocletian.

[4] Le Blanc, *Inscriptions chrétiennes de la Gaule*, II, lx, lxxi.

[5] Compare the use in the *limes* of Tripolitania at the end of the fourth century of Latin inscriptions which show clear signs of Christianity, and the probability that most Libyan inscriptions of the same date are pagan. See R. G. Goodchild, *BSR* XIX (1951), 78.

[6] Carcopino, *op. cit.* 298. The Arab invaders called them Romans.

Whether this is a legitimate conclusion or not, a further inscription[1] shows the relations between the Moorish inhabitants and the survivors of the romanized population. It is from Altava, and dated 508.

Pro sal(ute) et incol(umitate) reg(is) Masunae gentium Maur(orum) et Romanor(um) castrum edific(atum) a Masgivini pref(ecto) de Safari, Idir proc(uratore) castra Severiana quem Masuna Altava posuit. Et Maximus procurator Alt(avae) perfec(it). p(ositum) (anno) p(rovinciae) CCCCLXVIIII.

The places mentioned are in the region of Altava. The inscription is dated some twenty years after the revolt of the Moors against the Vandals, and eighty after the Vandal conquest. Although the king is a Moor and the Romans come in second place, their very mention, taken with the Roman character of the rest of the inscription, shows them to have been an important element. Masuna is mentioned by Procopius[2] as being, together with another chieftain called Ortaias, an ally of the Byzantines in their attempt to reconquer the Aures range in 535.

It is in precisely this latter area, so far from the west of Mauretania, yet in its mountainous regions apparently equally untouched by Rome, that a similar situation arose at exactly the same time. An inscription lately discovered in the north-west of the Aures shows this clearly.[3]

DMS. Ego Masties dux ann(is) LXVII et imp(erator) ann(is) XL qui nunquam perjuravi neque fide(m) fregi neque de Romanos neque de Mauros, et in bellu parui et in pace et adversus facta mea sic mecu(m) Deus egit bene. Ego Vartaia hunc edificum cum fratrib(us) (m)eis feci.

Vartaia is undoubtedly the same man as the Ortaias mentioned by Procopius, and was presumably a successor of Masties. In this inscription we have the same mention of Moors and Romans, with the latter having precedence, and the use of Roman titles. The assumption of the title *imperator* has been dated to 476,[4] the date of the disappearance of the last western emperor; this would make Masties *dux* in 449, a title perhaps given by Valentinian III who had nominal control over the Mauretanias and part of Numidia till 455. Such a dating would be an almost unique piece of evidence that the death of Romulus Augustulus had real significance at the time, and it is even more difficult to believe that it was noticed in the interior of the Vandal kingdom. This part of Numidia became independent of the Vandals in 484/5 at the earliest—

---

[1] *C* 9835.   [2] *De Bell. Vand.* II. 13. 19.   [3] *AE* (1945), 97.
[4] Carcopino in *Revue des études anciennes*, XLVI (1944), 116.

the appearance of Catholic bishops from Thabudeos and Thubunae at the conference of 484[1] being evidence for subjection at that date as in the case of the Mauretanian bishops. The title *imperator*, surely a demonstration of independence, might well be assumed by the leader of a revolt in which survivors of the romanized population played an important part. Masties would thus have been *dux* in 458 or later, perhaps a commission from Geiseric to defend the *limes* of southern Numidia. The use of Roman titles by the Vandals was nothing unusual, nor the employment of Moors.

These two inscriptions concerning Romano-Moorish kings, and the Christian epitaphs previously discussed, show how powerful was the attraction of Roman civilization and with it Christianity for the semi-barbarians of the African mountains. Romans they cannot be called either in the political or racial sense. They were practically untouched by colonization, their chief contacts with Roman influences being with the soldiers of the *limites* which surrounded the mountains —and this decreased with the barbarization of the army in the later Empire. While many Moors doubtless took the opportunity given by the Vandal invasion to gain their share of plunder, the benefits of the Roman régime with its peace and order were clearly remembered. This would have been particularly the case around the Aures with its prosperous fringe of *limitanei* dependent on settled conditions for the maintenance of their irrigation systems. It seems clear that it was at this very time that the threat of nomad incursions from the desert, which had been of small moment throughout the Roman period, became a permanent and dangerous feature of North African life through the greater use of camels by the inhabitants of the desert.[2]

Finally, it may be noted that the form of Christianity adopted by the Mauretanians was not Donatist but Catholic. No Donatist bishop or inscription is recorded further west than Ala Miliaria, to the east of the Chelif. The hundred and twenty Mauretanian Catholic bishops attending the conference of 484, perhaps half of whom came from west of the river, are conclusive evidence in this respect.

[1] Victor de Vita, *Notitia Episcoporum*, Numidia, 42 and 72 (*CSEL* VII, 120, 121); Procopius, *de Bell. Vand.* I. 8. 5.
[2] Gautier, *Les Siècles obscures du Mahgreb, passim*. Cf. Procopius, *de Bell. Vand.* III. 8. 5–29.

CHAPTER VII

DONATISM

THE ecclesiastical history of North Africa during the fourth century consists almost entirely of the struggle between the Catholic Church and the Donatist schism. The latter arose immediately after the great persecution of Diocletian; it grew rapidly and by the end of the century numbered in its congregation perhaps over half the Christians in Africa. The purpose of this chapter is to give a fairly full account of its origins and history,[1] with particular reference to its connexion with the political, social and economic history of North Africa.

At the time of Cyprian, Christianity was stronger in Africa than in any other western province. Besides the evidence for its flourishing condition found in the works of that writer we know that over eighty bishops attended the Council of Carthage in September 256.[2] The total number of African bishoprics was doubtless well over a hundred. Most of them were in the towns and cities, especially of Africa Proconsularis; the later development by which many *castella*, villages and even private chapels were served by bishops[3] had not yet made much progress. While Christianity was certainly strongest in the proconsular province there were also bishoprics in Numidia, some of them in the frontier regions.[4]

The period of peace between the edict of toleration granted by Gallienus in 260 and the persecution of Diocletian is as bare of documentary evidence for the spread of Christianity in Africa as it is in other provinces, but there can be no doubt that it made much progress. It is probable that the number of bishoprics doubled—in 312 there were at least seventy in Numidia alone, and by about 330, the Donatists could number two hundred and seventy.[5] Of the ten Numidian bishoprics

---

[1] This chapter was written before the appearance of the work of W. H. C. Frend, *The Donatist Church—a Movement of Protest in Roman North Africa*. For a full account of Donatism, see also vol. III of *Histoire littéraire de l'Afrique chrétienne* by Monceaux.

[2] *Sententiae episcoporum de haereticis baptizandis* (*CSEL* III, 436 ff.).

[3] *Gesta collationis Carthaginiensis*, Migne, *PL* XI, 1326. Both Catholics and Donatists allowed this practice.   [4] Badias (*Sentent.* 15), Gemellae (*Sentent.* 82).

[5] Aug. *Ep.* 93. 10. 43; Optatus, I. 18.

mentioned in the Acts of the Council of Cirta[1] (305), seven do not figure on documents from the time of Cyprian.[2] The increase seems to have been most marked in Numidia, and it is during this period that numbers of converts were made in the interior of the Mauretanias. In these provinces there had previously been few Christians and these were only in the coastal towns. In the persecution of Diocletian, there were martyrs at Oppidum Novum[3] and Tigava.[4] Owing to the custom in Mauretania of dating epitaphs and dedications by the provincial era, we can often closely date the appearance of Christianity in different regions. Epitaphs show Christians at Auzia in 318 and Altava in 302.[5] Many of these communities were small,[6] but it is clear that effective progress was being made in areas at best semi-barbarian.

It cannot be said that Christianity had advanced much amongst the wealthy and the educated. Doubtless a number of these, such as Tertullian, had been converted, and this continued in Diocletian's reign with Arnobius. But the majority of martyrs were from the lower classes. Among those of Abitina one is particularly mentioned as being a member of the town council, and one of the women as of good family,[7] but the rest were undistinguished, and some had native names. The Christianity of some women was violently rejected by the rest of their families.[8] The long peace and material prosperity of the Church, which we may deduce from the inventory of the property of the church at Cirta[9] in 303 and the concern of the bishop of Carthage for his church's wealth,[10] had an unfortunate effect on discipline. The true accounts of the martyrdoms show that the faith of some was firm and courageous. Nevertheless, the general picture of the African Church in the persecutions of 303–5 is one of weakness, from the bishops downwards,[11] especially in Numidia.

The end of the persecution in 305 brought the Church face to face with the problem of what was to be done about the *traditores*, those who had weakened in the face of danger to the extent of handing over the Scriptures to the authorities. A similar question had been the origin of

---

[1] Optatus, I. 13–14.   [2] Monceaux, *op. cit.* III, 5.
[3] *BAC* (1897), 573.   [4] *Passio Tipasii*, 8, in *Analect. Boll.* IX (1890), 116–23.
[5] *C* 20780 and 9862.   [6] *Passio Tipasii*, I.
[7] *Acta Saturnini*, 2 and 5 (*PL* VIII, 705–7).
[8] *Passio Maximae, Secundae et Donatillae*, 4, in *Analect. Boll.* IX (1890), 110–16.
[9] Appendix 1 to Optatus, *CSEL* XXVI, 187.
[10] Optatus, I. 17.   [11] Optatus, I. 13.

differences after the persecution of Decius in the time of Cyprian. Those who had suffered then were held in such high esteem, that the *lapsi* could claim readmission to the Church solely on the recommendation of a confessor. Cyprian was successful in avoiding a serious schism and in maintaining the authority of the episcopate without diminishing the glory of the confessors. It is not surprising that later, both Catholics and Donatists could find much in his life and writings to support their rival theses. After the persecution of Diocletian, the confessors went to the opposite extreme by refusing to communicate with *lapsi*. The passions aroused by this might have been overcome, as in the time of Cyprian, had not the greater part of the Numidian episcopate taken up the cause of the confessors. The motives of these bishops were doubtful. So far from being firm under persecution themselves, some, and the most influential, had weakened, and some were guilty of other crimes, ecclesiastical and civil.[1] By putting themselves at the head of those who resented any restrictions on the cult of the martyrs, they might well hope to remain in safety. The persecutions ended in 305, but there seems to have been no trouble for some years. This was doubtless partly due to the fact that there was still danger of the Numidians' weakness becoming known, partly to the political disturbances of the time. In 311/12, however, the bishop of Carthage died and a successor was quickly ordained without the customary presence of the primate of Numidia. The Numidian bishops seized upon this breach of tradition and seventy followed their primate and others whose guilty past might now be overlooked. When they arrived at Carthage, their objections to Caecilian, the new bishop, were no longer based upon traditional grounds (which would arouse no enthusiasm in Africa Proconsularis), but on the more popular cry that he had been ordained by a *traditor*, and that, since *traditores* were outside the Church, the ordination was invalid.[2] They then proceeded to ordain a rival bishop, Majorinus, who died within a short time of his election, and was succeeded by Donatus, called 'the Great', the man after whom the schism is named. He appears to have been born[3] in the town of Casae Nigrae on the

---

[1] *Gesta apud Zenophilum*, Appendix I to Optatus, *CSEL* xxvi, 192 ff. The authenticity of the documents in the appendix to Optatus seems now to be accepted. See Baynes, *Proceedings of the British Academy*, xv (1929), 413 f.

[2] Optatus, I. 18.

[3] Dom Chapman in *Revue bénédictine* (1909), 13–23, successfully asserts the identity of Donatus of Casae Nigrae and Donatus of Carthage.

Numidian frontier south-east of the Aures. He led the schism until his death c. 355.

Through its effect on St Augustine's thinking, Donatism had considerable, if indirect, influence on Catholic doctrine throughout the Middle Ages and even later, in particular on the Church's attitude towards the legitimacy of persecution of heresy and schism.[1] Donatism was also of importance in the social history of North Africa. It has been maintained[2] that it was in effect an attempt at social revolution by the lower classes, in particular the *coloni*, who naturally were by far the largest section of the population in that chiefly agricultural society. A viewpoint which approaches this is that the schism represented the growing assertiveness of the non-Roman (and non-romanized) population.[3] Since the agricultural population was the least romanized, social and racial animosities tended to coalesce into a solid support for Donatism against the Catholic Church which became associated with the imperial government and all its defects. Instances of religious divisions apparently being associated with various forms of discontent occur elsewhere in the ancient world.[4] What in origin was the exploitation of a genuine religious impulse by ambitious or guilty ecclesiastics, hardened with extraordinary rapidity into an organized church at least as numerous as its opponents. The enthusiasm which was evoked in the East by Christological disputes manifested itself in Africa in an extreme veneration of martyrs. The Donatist church was the church of the martyrs, not only in that it accorded great honour to canonical—and non-canonical—martyrs of the Diocletianic persecution, but also in that it cultivated with even more enthusiasm those of its own number who were killed after the beginning of the schism in disputes with the imperial authorities. More than this, suicide by a Donatist was accounted martyrdom.[5] The Donatists were the more successful in that they made no innovations in doctrine; all that they claimed was that the church of Majorinus, later of Donatus, was the true Catholic Church in Africa. This conservative attitude was a characteristic of Donatism

[1] E.g. the treatment of the Huguenots by Louis XIV was explicitly justified by reference to the persecution of the Donatists; see Sparrow Simpson, *St Augustine and African Church Divisions*, 147–50.

[2] Martroye, 'Une tentative de révolution sociale en Afrique, Donatistes et Circoncellions', in *Rev. quest. hist.* LXXVI (1904), 353–416 and LXXVII (1905), 1–53.

[3] Especially M. Thummel, *Zur Beurtheilung des Donatismus*.

[4] E.g. Nestorianism in Syria, Monophysitism in Egypt, in the sixth century.

[5] Aug. *contra Epist. Parmen.* I. 10. 16; *Ep.* 88. 8.

throughout its history, and cannot have been anything but popular among the rural and illiterate. Seventy Numidian bishops had accompanied Secundus of Tigisi to Carthage in 312; after the beginning of the schism more must have joined while in other sees opponents were set up against the Catholic occupants and by 330, the Donatists numbered at least 270 bishops.[1] The fact that Felix of Apthungi, who had ordained Caecilian, and on whose guilt as a *traditor* the Donatist case chiefly rested, was conclusively proved innocent,[2] had as little effect in slowing the advance as the publication of the guilt of their Numidian leaders; rather, the exile of the chief of these, Silvanus of Cirta, was represented as martyrdom.[3]

Long before this they had been subject to the first official action against schismatics or heretics taken by a Christian emperor. The speed with which Constantine acted in the dispute is evidence of the concern felt by the emperor, because of both his new religious convictions and the importance of keeping peace and order in Africa which was so vital to the food supply of Italy. The battle of the Milvian bridge had taken place on 28 October 312. During the same winter, letters from Constantine to the proconsul of Africa and to Caecilian himself reserved the restitution of properties confiscated during the persecutions, and granted immunities and other privileges to the Church led by Caecilian, and assured support by the proconsul and the vicar against his opponents.[4] By April 313 the schismatics found it necessary to appeal to the emperor. It is not necessary to enter into the details of the investigations which followed, both in Africa and elsewhere. Caecilian was vindicated by councils at Rome (313) and Arles (314), and by Constantine personally (November 316). Donatist basilicas and other property which the schismatics held were ordered to be handed over to the fiscus.[5] That the execution of this decree was expected to need force is shown by the fact that Ursacius, the commander of the troops in Africa, was associated with the vicar for the

[1] Aug. *Ep.* 93. 10. 43.
[2] Appendix II to Optatus, *CSEL* XXVI, 197 ff.
[3] Aug. *contra Cresconium*, III. 30. 34; the matter became public in 320.
[4] Aug. *Ep.* 93. 10. 43.
[5] It is possible that rather than issuing a decree condemning Donatism as such Constantine ordered them to be prosecuted for *calumnia* (Martroye, 'La répression du Donatisme', in *Mémoires de la Société des antiquaires de France*, LXIII (1913), 24). But see N. H. Baynes, 'Constantine the Great and the Christian Church', in *Proceedings of the British Academy*, XV (1929), 354 and 418.

purpose.[1] Violence was chiefly confined to Carthage,[2] and some Donatists were killed, to be subsequently honoured as martyrs. The schism survived, however; numerous pamphlets attacking Catholics for betrayal evoked a law ordering the authorities to disregard them.[3] In 321 the Donatist exiles appealed to Constantine to suspend the measures being taken against them. The matter had by now become distasteful to the emperor and politically disadvantageous as well, owing to his worsening relations with Licinius; the exiles were permitted to return. This was a simple act of clemency; the confiscated basilicas were not given back to the Donatists, but it may safely be assumed that they remained in possession in many places where the execution of the decree of 316 had not been firmly carried out. Constantine ended his letter informing the vicar of Africa of the pardon by leaving the punishment of the schism to God.[4]

Donatism was thus left to grow almost unchecked. The Catholics realized that Constantine had in effect washed his hands of the affair, since in 322 he wrote advising moderation.[5] In Numidia the dissidents were so strong that by 330 they took possession of the basilica at Constantine,[6] which the emperor had ordered to be built for the Catholics, and in spite of the fact that the city was now the place of residence of the provincial governor. They had further been able by some means to force some of the Catholic clergy there into the *curia* against the law of 326.[7] Constantine allowed the schismatics to retain possession of the basilica, merely providing another for the Catholics, and reaffirming clerical immunity from municipal charges except in the case of schismatics and heretics. About 330, a Donatist council met in Carthage, and decided, among other things, on the initiative of the Mauretanian bishops, to admit Catholics into their Communion without a second baptism.[8] This, though against the Donatist principle that they alone, being the true Catholic Church and the Church of the

---

[1] *Passio Donati*, 2 (*PL* VIII, 753).

[2] *Passio Donati*, 2–3; Aug. *contra Epist. Parmen.* I. 8. 13.

[3] *Cod. Theod.* IX. 34. 1 (319).

[4] 'Ad Valerium vicarium de illorum exilio soluto et eorum furore Deo vindici dimittendo litteras dedit.' Aug. *ad Donatistas post collationem* XXXIII. 56.

[5] Appendix IX to Optatus, *CSEL* XXVI, 212.

[6] Appendix X to Optatus, *CSEL* XXVI, 215.

[7] 'Privilegia, quae contemplatione religionis indulta sunt, catholicae tantum legis observatoribus prodesse oportet'; *Cod. Theod.* XVI. 5. 1.

[8] Aug. *Ep.* 93. 10. 43.

Saints, could give effective baptism, was of great assistance in widening their influence.

Before the Peace of the Church there had been few basilicas, at least of any size. After the end of the persecution, however, there was no restraint and in Africa the division in the Church meant that there was more incentive than in other provinces towards the erection of basilicas. Although only a few can be accurately dated, and in many cases we have no means of knowing whether they were Donatist or Catholic, there are sufficient which are certainly of the fourth century to indicate that a considerable amount of money and labour was spent by both Churches on their buildings.

At the town of Castellum Tingitanum, in Mauretania Caesariensis, was a basilica which can be dated to 324,[1] the earliest yet discovered in North Africa. The building was of a fair size and the floor was entirely covered with mosaics of a high standard.[2] This basilica was almost certainly a Catholic one, but at the end of the fourth century a chapel containing relics of SS. Peter and Paul was built nearby which was probably Donatist.[3] The chapel dedicated to St Salsa at Tipasa, on the coast of the same province, is also of the early fourth century. In the interior of the province, the Donatist church at Ala Miliaria, a small fortified town, dates from about 430. Nothing remains of the churches of Caesarea, the capital of the province, but there were several at the time of St Augustine including at least two belonging to the Catholics.[4]

Churches or chapels in Mauretania Sitifensis which can be even broadly dated are lacking. It is probable, however, that the building of two basilicas in several villages and small fortified towns which can only have had small populations attests the rivalry between Donatists and Catholics which was very strong in this area.[5] Optatus reproached the Donatists for having built 'unnecessary basilicas'.[6] Examples are to be found at Kherbet bou Addoufen, Hr. bou Takramatĕne and Kherbet Selmi, all within a short distance of Sitifis.

In Numidia most of the larger places had churches by the time of St Augustine, and many had two as a result of the schism. Cirta had

---

[1] C 9708.
[2] Gsell, Monuments antiques de l'Algérie, II, 240.
[3] C 9714, 9715; W. H. C. Frend, JRS xxx (1940), 32.
[4] De Gestis cum Emerito I (PL XLIII, 697). The meeting between Augustine and Emeritus took place 'in ecclesia majori'.
[5] Gsell, Monuments, II, 117.   [6] Optatus, III. 1.

had a basilica even before the persecution of Diocletian. The basilica at Cuicul, which probably dates from the beginning of the fifth century, was erected at the expense of some former imperial officials of high rank.[1] At the Conference of Carthage in 411, the Donatist bishop of Milev was accused of having destroyed four basilicas in one place[2]—perhaps Milev itself. At Vegesela was a basilica of considerable size, well decorated and containing relics of the Donatist martyr, Marculus.[3] It is probably to be dated to the years between 347 and 362. Lastly, in the villages along the plateau to the north of the Aures have been found[4] numbers of small churches and chapels in which the cult centred around the veneration of relics. Although the possession of relics of a martyr was not necessarily the mark of a Donatist basilica, the discovery of inscriptions[5] known to be Donatist at or near some of these sites and the fact that the majority of identifiable places in the area were represented by unopposed Donatist bishops in 411 lead inevitably to the conclusion that most of these buildings were Donatist and of the fourth century.

In the Proconsular province, the position was somewhat different. Although the Catholics were stronger than the Donatists, the influence of paganism was also still considerable. Many of the towns had indeed been bishoprics at the time of Cyprian, and a much larger number had this distinction at the beginning of the fifth century; but in some of the towns Christianity was certainly weak. For instance, in Thibilis and the much larger town of Thuburscicu Numidarum no Christian buildings or even epitaphs of this period have been found in very thorough investigations.[6] In some places, however, where Christianity was strong, we find the most considerable Christian remains in North Africa. The supremacy of Carthage in this respect is natural because of her wealth and ecclesiastical position. Unfortunately, though the Christian epigraphy of Carthage is very rich, the remains of the churches are scanty, owing to long occupation of the sites. It is the city of Theveste, close to the Numidian border, which provides the finest surviving example of a fourth-century basilica in Africa. Its size and richness of ornament

---

[1] C 8344–8, including a *v.c. ex principe* (8344) and a *v.c. ex tribuno* (8345).
[2] *PL* XI, 1339.
[3] P. Cayrel, *Mél. d'arch. et d'hist.* LI (1934), 114 ff.
[4] A. Berthier, *Les Vestiges du Christianisme dans la Numidie antique.*
[5] E.g. C 18660, 10694, 17768, 2308.
[6] Both places were, however, bishoprics in 411.

are remarkable. The main part is dated to the period immediately after the victory of the Church, and some considerable enlargements to the later fourth century.[1] From the works of St Augustine we learn that at Hippo Regius there were three Catholic basilicas, one built by Augustine himself, two chapels, and a Donatist basilica.[2] It is probable that had we the literary sources we would find this multiplicity in other places, especially in coastal cities like Hippo Regius, Carthage and Hadrumetum where Christianity had been longest established. At Thamugadi, where the conflict between the two Churches was very bitter, there were no fewer than seventeen churches, chapels and monasteries of varying dates and allegiance.[3] Thus, even while reserves are made in the question of dating the basilicas, the number that were constructed is remarkable, even in rural districts where enthusiasm for one or other of the rival Churches made up for an apparent lack of material resources. This may finally be illustrated by an inscription[4] found some miles east of Thamugadi showing how three villages joined together to build and decorate their basilica:

(basilic)am no(vam) Venusianenses initiaverunt, Mucrionenses columnas V dederunt Cuzabetenses dederunt columnas VI omnes apsida straverunt, plus Cuzabetenses ornaverunt.

It is Optatus of Milev writing between 364 and 376 in answer to the pamphlet of Parmenian, Donatist bishop of Carthage, who provides our earliest reference to the class of people known as *circumcelliones*, who, owing to their association with the schismatics, figure so frequently in the polemics of St Augustine and in modern interpretations of the social role of Donatism. They are described by Augustine in the following words: 'genus hominum...maxime in agris territans et victus sui causa cellas circumiens rusticanas, unde circumcellionum nomen accipit'.[5] Isidore of Seville says they get the name 'quod agrestes sunt'.[6] Both these descriptions indicate that they were no more than agricultural labourers of a sort. *Cellae* are almost certainly barns, storehouses and so on. While Cassiodorus[7] and Isidore[8] (in another work)

---

[1] Gsell, *Monuments*, II, 275. [2] References in Gsell, *ibid.* 213.
[3] Mesnage, *L'Afrique chrétienne*, 387.
[4] *AE* (1894), 25 and 138. There is nothing to tell whether this was Catholic or Donatist. The Donatist bishop of Cusabeta was unopposed at the conference of Carthage (411); the other villages are unknown.
[5] *Contra Gaudentium*, I. 28. 32. [6] *Etym.* 8 5. 53.
[7] *In. ps.* 132. 1. [8] *Eccl. off.* II. 16. 7.

imply that the *circumcelliones* were monks of a sort, presumably taking *cellae* to mean monasteries, it seems that this meaning of the word does not occur till the fifth century.[1] That they were solidly Donatist and comprised the most extreme members of the sect is certain. About 340 two men named Axido and Fasir led bands of *circumcelliones* through part of Numidia, committing acts primarily directed against the rich; no creditor could attempt to get his money back without being threatened by them; even the roads were unsafe, and slaves rode in their masters' carriages while the masters were forced to walk behind. Axido and Fasir were called by their followers 'leaders of the Saints',[2] thus showing their adherence to the Donatists who considered themselves to be 'Sancti'.[3] The Donatist bishops, however, were so disturbed by this violence which they were unable to control that they requested armed assistance from Count Taurinus. Numbers of *circumcelliones* were killed at Octava in southern Numidia; they were subsequently honoured by the Donatists as martyrs, in spite of the fact that it was the Donatist bishops who had called for the suppression.

The *circumcelliones* were responsible for further violence seven years later when, under the leadership of the Donatist bishop of Bagai (likewise in southern Numidia) they resisted the troops escorting the commissioners sent by Constans to unify the Churches. According to Optatus it was from among the *circumcelliones* that the false martyrs of Donatism who threw themselves over cliffs usually came. The violence of the *circumcelliones* seems to have been sporadic. The repression which followed the breach of public order in Numidia (which might have threatened the *annona*) may have been responsible for their subsequent quietness; even in the years following 362 when the return of Donatist exiles brought with it much religious violence they do not appear to have been troublesome, for Optatus, writing as an eyewitness and a controversialist only a few years after this, must have mentioned the fact had they broken out. On the other hand, references to the *circumcelliones* in the letters and polemical works of Augustine are extraordinarily numerous. It is certain that in the last years of the fourth century they were a more serious threat to public order than before. In the first place, in addition to their acts of violence, Augustine continually stressed and clearly disliked the fact that they wandered

[1] *Thesaurus ling. Lat.* s.v. *cella.*   [2] 'Duces Sanctorum', Optatus, III. 4.
[3] Optatus, II. I. 14. 20.

over the countryside, and were not fixed to any place.[1] After 411, and the beginning of the effective use of secular power against the schismatics, he wrote of the numerous *circumcelliones* 'who are now kept in order, and are attached to the soil, having given up both the name and the occupation of *circumcelliones*'.[2] Associated with this was the fact that the wandering bands were of both sexes, and Augustine many times attacked their sexual immorality.[3] Leaders of the *circumcelliones* were often Donatist priests and they used the Donatist slogan 'laus deo'. Augustine, like Optatus, also ridiculed the voluntary martyrdoms in which they indulged.[4]

When it comes to exposing their acts of violence, Augustine is inexplicit. By far the greater number of references to crimes committed by *circumcelliones* are in general terms; for example: 'Many crimes are daily committed by wild bands of drunken young men, led by Donatist priests; at first they carried only sticks but now have begun to arm themselves with swords. They wander and commit violence over the whole of Africa against all the authority of the law.'[5] On another occasion they are said to commit worse crimes than thieves and bandits; the crimes seem to have been principally housebreaking, arson, and assault (including blinding) upon Catholic priests.[6] Similar crimes are recorded where laymen were the victims.[7] This is hardly violence on a scale amounting to a revolt requiring substantial military force to repress it, as in the case of the Bagaudae in Gaul. There is no need to minimize the atmosphere of intimidation which the *circumcelliones* obviously produced in places where they were numerous; but Augustine would certainly have made full use of any particularly violent crime alleged to have been committed by them if he had known of one. Outrages against Christians by pagan crowds are more exactly described in his letters.[8]

It has been argued[9] on the basis of their violent behaviour that while admittedly being rural workers of a sort, as described by Augustine in the passage quoted above, companies of *circumcelliones* were made up of

---

[1] E.g. *contra Gaudentium*, I. 28. 32; *contra Epist. Parmen.* I. 11. 17, II. 3. 6; *contra Litt. Pet.* II. 87. 195; *Ep. ad Cath.* 19. 50.   [2] *Contra Gaudentium*, I. 28. 33.
[3] *Contra Epist. Parmen.* III. 3. 18, *Ep. ad Cath.* 19. 50.
[4] *Contra Epist. Parmen.* II. 3. 6; *contra Litt. Pet.* II. 88. 195.
[5] *Contra Epist. Parmen.* I. 11. 17.   [6] *Contra Cresconium*, III. 42. 46.
[7] *Ad Donatistas post collat.* 17. 22.
[8] Aug. *Ep.* 50 (399), on the massacre of sixty Christians at Sufes (in Byzacena); *Ep.* 91 (408), a church at Calama burnt and a priest killed.   [9] Monceaux, *op. cit.* IV. 190.

fugitive slaves, ruined *coloni* and disaffected members of barbarian tribes. It seems more likely, however, that the *circumcelliones* were a distinct social class, and recognized as such by law.[1] A constitution issued in 412,[2] the outcome of the conference of Carthage which finally condemned Donatism, gave a scale of penalties to be paid by persons who refused to give up the schism as follows:

Inlustres	50 pounds of gold	
Spectabiles	40 ,,	,,
Senatores	30 ,,	,,
Clarissimi	20 ,,	,,
Sacerdotales	30 ,,	,,
Municipales	20 ,,	,,
Decuriones	5 ,,	,,
Negotiatores	5 ,,	,,
Plebei	5 ,,	,,
Circumcelliones	10 pounds of silver	
Servi	*admonitio* by their masters	
Coloni	Corporal punishment	

This law was repeated almost word for word, with the substitution of Catholics for Donatists as the victims, by the Vandal king Hunneric in 484.[3]

We can hardly suppose that the emperors have been forced to recognize groups of fugitives as a social class. In this law, they rank as the highest group of the rural population (*plebei* are inhabitants of the towns). Further, they do not suffer the personal punishment of the servile or semi-servile, and are consequently a class of free men. We learn also that they were under the supervision of *conductores* who had the responsibility of bringing them to justice, had seizable property, and worked on both imperial and private estates.

Neither Optatus nor Augustine mentions the social position of the *circumcelliones*. But since both emphasize their nomadic character, we may say that they were free, agricultural workers who went from estate to estate offering their labour. Such a class of people had long been known in Africa.[4] Their general attachment to Donatism and

---

[1] Cp. Saumagne, *Ann. d'hist. éc. et soc.* VI (1934), 35 ff.

[2] *Cod. Theod.* XVI. 5. 52.   [3] Victor de Vita, III. 3.

[4] E.g. *C* 11824, probably of the third century, a long inscription relating how such a free workman eventually became *censor* of his city. It may be noted that, though his home was in Byzacena, he worked in Numidia (ll. 10 and 16) where the *circumcelliones* were afterwards most numerous.

increasing violence very likely result from pressure by the authorities and the landowners to fix them to the soil; a change of status would soon mean loss of personal freedom. That this was a solution approved by Augustine is shown in a passage already quoted.[1] They appear to have been numerous almost exclusively in those districts such as southern Numidia[2] and near Hippo Regius,[3] where large estates were numerous and where they could thus expect work. There is no record of them in Mauretania where agriculture on a large scale was lacking.

The *circumcelliones* were thus a class which was almost entirely attached to Donatism. Other sections of the community were divided, but there are numerous references which prove conclusively that the Donatists were strongest in Numidia,[4] where there were few towns of any size. The number of Donatist bishops from identified places in this province and from the southern part of Mauretania Sitifensis (which had the same characteristics) who were present unopposed by Catholics at the Conference of Carthage testifies to the same fact.[5] There can be no doubt that many of these bishops came from small villages and *castella* on imperial or private estates, inhabited almost entirely by *coloni*.[6] Whether the adherence of the rural population in these parts to Donatism was entirely due to discontent with their lot is another matter; though doubtless, as conditions during the century gradually deteriorated, and exploitation by officials and landowners grew more prevalent, such a motive became prominent especially when the oppressors were Catholics or acting for Catholic emperors. But when the schism started, at least seventy bishops from Numidia joined it at once for the most varied of reasons, which are discussed above.[7] For their congregations there can have been no choice; they automatically became members of the *pars Donati*.[8] The blindness with which the people followed their bishops is indicated by the attitude of even a well-educated man, the grammarian Victor of Cirta.[9] It must have been long before the Catholics could form fresh congregations in

---

[1] *Contra Gaudentium*, I. 28. 33; above, p. 86.

[2] Optatus, III. 4.   [3] Aug. *Ep*. 108. 5. 14.

[4] E.g. Aug. *Ep*. 58; *Sermo*, 46. 15. 39; *Gesta coll. Carth.* I. 165; *Ep. ad Cath.* 19. 51.

[5] See W. H. C. Frend, *JRS* xxx (1940), 39. It is true that the non-appearance of an opponent at the conference is not necessarily proof that there was none, but the evidence for Donatist preponderance here is very strong. See also above, p. 80.

[6] *Gesta coll. Carth.* I. 181.

[7] Pp. 78 f.   [8] Optatus, III. 3.

[9] *Gesta apud Zenophilum*, Appendix I to Optatus, *CSEL* xxvi, 185.

even the larger of these places, and we have no means of knowing how many other bishops with their people went over to the schism in its early years for motives entirely of conscience. This early extension of the schism into the interior of Africa also meant that many of the rustic pagans who were converted during the fourth century became Donatists because only this form of Christianity was known to them.

The agricultural basis of society was as marked in Proconsularis and Byzacena as it was in Numidia, though civic life was much more developed. In the former, Donatism was always weaker than Catholicism; in the latter the Churches were about equal in strength.[1] In 312 it was the supporters of Caecilian who were in possession of the bishoprics and the churches' property, and it was for the Donatists to prove that they alone were the true church. Thus the Catholics had the initiative as the Donatists had it in Numidia. Doubtless also the standard of life among the rural population in the Proconsular province at least was higher than on the high plains of Numidia nor could the ameliorative effect of city life be valueless. There were, therefore, several factors working against the spread of Donatism in this part of Africa.

Augustine states that Latin and 'Punic'[2] were the two languages in use amongst the Donatists, and from other references in his works to the latter tongue, it has been thought that we have here proof of the position enjoyed by the schismatics among the non-romanized population. Many of these references are concerned with the district around Hippo Regius, precisely where numerous Libyan inscriptions have been found.[3] The archaeological atlas shows that in the vicinity of that city the mountainous districts were almost untouched by Roman civilization.[4] Augustine when choosing a priest for some village in this region naturally sought one with a knowledge of the native tongue. Yet there is no evidence of widespread use of these languages among the

---

[1] Augustine, writing just before the conference of 411, states that the Catholics were more numerous in all the provinces except Numidia (*Ep.* 129. 6). He may have been exaggerating here (though persecution was already affecting Donatist strength); the schismatics had over a hundred bishops in Byzacena.

[2] *In Johannis Ep.* 11. 3. There is little doubt that all non-Latin languages in Africa were grouped together by Augustine as Punic. The true Punic language was more or less confined to the coastal cities, while in the interior, various Libyan dialects were spoken. See Chabot, *Receuil des inscriptions libyques.*

[3] E.g. *Ep.* 108. 5. 14 and *Ep.* 209; *ILAlg* 137, 138, 141, 145, 153, etc.

[4] Gsell, *Atlas arch. Alg.* s.v. Hippo Regius.

clergy of either Church. The Donatist opponent of Augustine at Hippo Regius was as ignorant of it as the saint himself.[1] The same applies to the Donatist bishop of Calama (whose *coloni*, though 'Punic'-speaking, were Catholic).[2] It is thus unwise to read too much into Augustine's general statement about the use of the African language. Doubtless it was used in places by both Churches; but the difficulty experienced by Augustine in finding a priest to speak it shows how it had dropped out of use among those of even the slightest education. The learned leaders of the Donatists, with their chief of Gallic or Spanish origin, were certainly ignorant of it.

In the Mauretanias Roman civilization was practically confined to the cities of the long sea coast, the valley of the Chelif, and the plains round Sitifis. There were also considerable areas in which native tribes were left in almost complete independence. It seems clear that Christianity of either division made slow progress in these provinces (except round Sitifis) in the fourth century. Augustine wrote[3] in 418 that innumerable barbarians in Africa had never heard the gospel; in the few years immediately before he was writing, a few belonging to tribes within the borders of the African provinces had been converted and the *praefecti* set over such tribes were just beginning to be Christian. As for the tribes outside the frontiers, they were entirely pagan. We may also compare the number of bishoprics recorded in these provinces in 411[4] and 484.[5] The figures for Mauretania Sitifensis are 27 and 44, for Caesariensis 28 and 120. The latter figure is the more remarkable in that large parts of Caesariensis can have been only weakly held by the Vandals in 484 and the bishops were not likely to have been keen to attend a council the outcome of which was a foregone conclusion.[6] Some Moorish tribes remained pagan during the fifth century[7] despite the rapid progress of Christianity during that time.

The Catholics seem to have been as strong as, if not stronger than, the Donatists in the Mauretanias, except round Sitifis. There were no Donatists in Mauretania Tingitana, though they appeared in the others at an early date.[8] Emeritus of Caesarea became one of the leaders of the schism at the time of Augustine; but it is significant that his see was the

---

[1] Aug. *Ep.* 108. 5. 14.   [2] Aug. *Ep.* 66. 2.   [3] *Ep.* 199. 12. 46.

[4] Computed from the identifiable sees represented at the Conference of Carthage at this date.

[5] Lists of bishoprics, the *Notitia Episcoporum*, in Victor de Vita, *CSEL* VII. 117 ff.

[6] Victor de Vita, III. 1.   [7] Victor de Vita, I. 35–7.   [8] Aug. *Ep.* 93. 10. 43.

capital of the province and one of the largest cities in Africa. It was Donatists from Numidia who were responsible for violence in Mauretania in 362. The extraordinary number of bishops from Mauretania Caesariensis in 484 shows that the form of Christianity adopted there was Catholic. The events in which Firmus and Gildo played a part do not prove the contrary. Their father Nubel was a Christian and very probably orthodox, if an inscription found at Rusguniae[1] refers to him. Gildo's daughter and aunt were later renowned for their sanctity in Catholic circles.[2] One of his brothers, Sammac, erected an inscription on his estate boasting of his loyalty to Rome.[3] On the other hand, Firmus both received help from and assisted the Donatists on particular occasions. The Donatist bishop of Rusubbicari, a coastal town of Mauretania, betrayed the place to Firmus on the understanding that his congregation would not suffer pillage.[4] His estimate of the character of Firmus' Moorish troops is obvious. Later, Firmus persecuted the Rogatists, a local subdivision of the Donatists.

The outburst of Moorish national feeling, if such it was, was short-lived and dependent on the character and position of Firmus. His brother, Gildo, who served Rome as *comes Africae* between 387 and 398, was more obviously linked with the Donatists, especially in Numidia.[5] Yet, when he revolted, he seems to have had little support from the tribes, and was defeated almost without bloodshed at his very first meeting with the imperial troops.

Very little is known of the expansion of Donatism among the upper classes in the towns. It is certainly true that these were long attached to paganism,[6] and in Africa Proconsularis at least, where they were Christian, were principally Catholic. That Donatism did make considerable headway among the educated is, however, clear from our knowledge of the careers of some of its leading figures. Donatus himself, besides being a man of great force of character, was recognized by his opponents as a man with a sound knowledge of 'profane letters'.[7] This indicates an education in the traditional Roman manner, which

---

[1] *C* 9255.
[2] Jerome, *Ep.* 79, to Salvina, daughter of Gildo. She was the widow of Nebridius, the nephew of Theodosius.
[3] *CRAI* (1901), 170.   [4] Aug. *Ep.* 87. 10.
[5] Aug. *contra Litt. Pet.* II, *passim*; *Ep.* 87. 10. His activity was mostly against the divisions of Donatism, not the Catholics.
[6] Above, p. 36.   [7] Optatus, III. 3, 'scientia mundanarum litterarum'.

flourished in the African towns right through the fourth century.[1] Tyconius, the most original thinker of the schism, was brought up as a Donatist; he was also fully educated in the traditional studies and in religious matters.[2] St Augustine himself did not think it unfitting to adapt some of his thought.[3] The curious story of Petilian shows how all classes had accepted the schism. He was a lawyer of great reputation at Constantine. Although a Catholic, he was ordained bishop against his will by the Donatists. Instead of repudiating this, he devoted the rest of his life and his brilliant talents to his new faith and became its chief spokesman.[4] Cresconius,[5] a lay grammarian and Donatist apologist, and Emeritus,[6] bishop of Caesarea, are both commended by Augustine as men of education. Such is the abundance of Donatist literature, compared with that from the Catholic side before Augustine, that were this our only evidence we might suppose that Catholicism was the religion of the unlettered, while Donatism had won over the educated. It is clear that for much of the fourth century Donatism attracted the best intellects among the African Christians. Lawyers and grammarians came chiefly from the class of *curiales*—though they themselves might obtain immunity from civic duties—and we may conclude that the intellectual leadership of the Donatists was derived from the same source.

The highest classes of society from *clarissimi* upwards were included among those threatened with fines for persistence in Donatism.[7] A certain Celer, proconsul of Africa in 427, had in his early life been a Donatist.[8] That Church itself had considerable property and it was common for schismatics to bequeath their wealth to it.[9] Nevertheless, it is clear from the numerous references in St Augustine that at the end of the fourth century these persons were mostly either pagan or Catholic. To deal only with the latter, there are several letters of Augustine encouraging Catholic landowners to persuade their *coloni* to give up Donatism.[10]

The attitude of the successors of Constantine to the schism may be

---

[1] See below, Ch. VIII.   [2] Gennadius, *de Vir. ill.* 18.

[3] *De Doctrina Christ.* III. 30. See also *Ep.* 41. 2.

[4] Aug. *Sermo ad Caesariensis Eccl. plebem*, 8; *contra Litt. Pet.* I. 1.

[5] Aug. *contra Cresconium*, I. 2. 3.   [6] Aug. *Ep.* 87. 1. 3.

[7] *Cod. Theod.* XVI. 5. 52 (412).   [8] Aug. *Epp.* 56 and 57.

[9] Aug. *contra Epist. Parmen.* I. 12. 19. The person here mentioned was the sister of a 'homo nobilis'.

[10] E.g. *Epp.* 58, 89, 112.

briefly considered as it throws light on the economic importance of Africa as well as providing an example of the weakness of the later imperial administration. In 347 the first serious attempt at repression was made. Constans sent two commissioners, Paul and Macarius, to unite the Churches by persuasion, by assisting the Catholics financially and presumably by bribing the Donatist leaders.[1] Whether an order was issued at the very beginning condemning Donatism may be doubt-ful.[2] In the Donatist *Passio Marculi* it is stated that in the provinces other than Numidia Macarius proceeded with subtlety, using force only in the latter.[3] Use of physical repression seems to have been subsequent to the violence offered to the commissioners by Donatus of Bagai and the *circumcelliones*. As a result of this the Donatists were subjected to a long and violent persecution; whoever was suspected of complicity with the *circumcelliones* was hunted down. This particularly injured the Donatist clergy. Many schismatic communities were dissolved as a result of the flight or the exile of their leaders.[4] The *circumcelliones* were guilty of the serious crime of *seditio*, armed action against the state. Macarius was, however, guilty of an abuse of *coercitio*, the power of administrative action without recourse to the courts which was allowed magistrates in such cases.[5] Corporal punishment and exile[6] were penalties which he inflicted and which constituted an abuse of this power. The action of Macarius was one on which St Augustine evidently had some reserves.[7]

The Catholics were now supreme in Africa. Through force in Numidia, through less obvious pressure in other provinces, the Dona-tists had been dispersed. Donatus himself and many other leaders were exiled. The period between 347 and 362 was considered by Optatus an age of gold;[8] a Catholic council was held in Carthage in 348 to

---

[1] Optatus, III. 3–4.

[2] Optatus, III. 3; 'Quis negare potest Constantem... Paulum et Macarium primitus non ad faciendum unitatem misisse sed cum eleemosynis?' Cf. Martroye, 'La répression du donatisme', *Mém. Soc. antiq. France*, LXXIII, 61 ff.

[3] *PL* VIII, 761.   [4] Optatus, III. 1.

[5] Martroye, *op. cit.* 71.   [6] *Passio Marculi* (*PL* VIII, 762).

[7] *Psalmus contra partem Donati*, 144–6 (*PL* XLIII, 28):

  'Modum si excessit Macarius conscriptum in Christiana lege
  Vel legem regis referebat, ut pugnaret pro unitate:
  Non dico istum nihil peccasse, sed vestros peiores esse.'

Ibid. 158:

  'Si crudeles erant illi [e.g. Macarius et Paulus] et nobis displicent valde.'

[8] Optatus, II. 15.

consolidate the victory, moderation was enjoined and even practised. During the next fourteen years, while the rest of the Christian world was absorbed in the Arian controversy, Africa was quiet.

The only evidence for an attempt at an understanding between Donatus and the Arians dates from before the mission of Paul and Macarius. The Eastern Council of Serdica had sent a copy of its proceedings to Donatus, and he himself wrote in 345 a work on the Trinity which was considered to approach the Arian viewpoint.[1] Whether this had any bearing on the actual date of the mission cannot be determined. Athanasius had re-entered Alexandria in triumph in 346; possibly the Catholic party at Constans' court pressed for a gesture which would likewise show their triumph over Arians or potential Arians in the West. In fact, the Donatists in Africa remained strictly orthodox in their theology in the sense of adopting nothing which had not been of the faith at the close of the great persecution.

The popularity of Donatism and its continued strength despite the dispersion of its leaders were revealed during the reign of Julian. Some of the exiled clergy appealed to the emperor to extend to them the decrees in favour of Christians who had been exiled by Constantius. They obtained a rescript giving restitution of everything of which they had been deprived without proper justification.[2] This meant the basilicas and other properties which had been taken from those exiled or imprisoned by Macarius in excess of his authority. They received also the same right of freedom of worship as was granted to other sects. Julian's motive was, of course, to weaken orthodox Christianity by allowing the schisms and heresies to flourish.

The revival of Donatism was marked by much violence. In this case it was not the *circumcelliones* who were to blame but the returning clergy who excited their congregations in many cases to anticipate the due processes of law which would restore their property. Known instances of violence took place in all parts of Africa, Carpi (Proconsularis), Tisedi (Numidia), Lemellef (Sitifensis) and Tipasa (Caesariensis).[3] At the last-named place there is the first record of partiality towards the Donatists not only by officials, but by the governor himself. These,

[1] Jerome, *de Vir. ill.* 93.
[2] Aug. *contra Litt. Pet.* II. 97, 224; '. . .ut abolitis quae adversus eos sine rescripto perperam gesta sunt in antiquum statum cuncta revocentur'.
[3] Optatus, II. 18 and 19.

almost certainly pagans and in sympathy with Julian, did not intervene when a Donatist mob attacked the Catholics.[1]

The situation was adversely reported by other governors,[2] but there is no record of any strong action taken to stop the disorders. The mind of the emperor was too well known; the governors were mostly, or all, still pagans, and unlikely to risk their careers or more over such an issue.

The reign of Julian and the violence of the Donatists were short. With the accession of Jovian and, soon after, Valentinian, the supreme power returned to Christians. The Donatists took to the slower but safer methods of the law courts to regain their property. Such a change would commend itself to Parmenian, the new Donatist bishop of Carthage who was known to all as a moderate man, if fully determined about the rightness of his cause. Parmenian was, in fact, of Spanish or Gallic origin, yet succeeded Donatus while still in exile, and led his party with as much energy as his predecessor. The external origin of the leader of a purely African schism was a matter for comment in his own lifetime.[3] He was presumably converted to Donatism by a sincere belief in its claim to be the true Church, and had little sympathy for the extreme element in Africa.

The religious policy of Valentinian, which was to allow freedom to all to worship as they wished,[4] applied to the Donatists for the first part of his reign. Only after the revolt of Firmus (372–4) did the series of laws, extending over forty years and ending in the victory of Catholicism, if not in the complete dissolution of Donatism, begin. The campaign against Firmus had been long and difficult, and although it had not spread outside Mauretania into Numidia where the Donatists were strongest, the schismatics had clearly allied themselves with the rebel. This made their punishment a necessity for the safety of the other provinces.

The first law proscribing the sect was dated 17 October 377[5] and addressed to the vicar of Africa, Flavianus. Abandoning the policy of Valentinian I (who had died in 375) the emperors began with an

---

[1] Optatus, II. 18; 'nonnullorum officialium et favore et furore juvante et Athenio praeside praesente cum signis'.

[2] Optatus, II. 17.   [3] Optatus, II. 7.

[4] *Cod. Theod.* IX. 16. 9; '...unicuique, quod animo inbibisset, colendi libera facultas tributa est'.

[5] *Cod. Theod.* XVI. 6. 2.

outright condemnation of the errors of the Donatists and required them to hand over their basilicas to the Catholics and rural meeting-places to the fiscus.

The identity of the official to whom the law was addressed provides the answer to the question why even at this stage so much legislation against the sect was ineffective. Flavianus was afterwards celebrated for his benevolent attitude towards the Donatists;[1] he himself was a staunch pagan,[2] a cousin of Symmachus. His activity in Africa is typical of the negligence or worse by which provincial governors and other high officials thwarted the wishes of emperors in the later part of the fourth century. The vicars and governors of the African provinces, drawn as they usually were from the Roman aristocracy, were mostly pagan to a very late date. The first proconsul of Africa known to have been a Christian was Sex. Petronius Probus[3] (358): the next was Constantius[4] (374) otherwise unknown. He was followed by the son and the son-in-law of Ausonius, probably no more than 'half-Christians' like the poet. The pagan panegyrist Pacatus Drepanius governed the province in 390, and an apostate, Marcianus, in 394, presumably on behalf of the usurper Eugenius. Christians again appear in 396[5] and 397,[6] but as late as 410, one of the last known proconsuls was Macrobius, the pagan author of the *Saturnalia*. In Numidia, the predominance of pagans is still more marked—though the number of governors known to us is smaller than that for Proconsularis, and it may be that some whose names are lost were Christians. As it is, however, the first known Christian governor of Numidia held office as late as 410.[7] Pagans were vicars of Africa in 380/1[8] and 391/3[9] with only a possible Christian *c.* 385.[10] Those governors who were honest enough not to use the weakness of the central power to their own advantage often interpreted the imperial constitutions in a way suited to their own opinions. In many cases, self-interest required such caution; changes of policy at the court were frequent and too enthusiastic a governor might face awkward questions on his return. It was only when the officials and

[1] Aug. *Ep.* 87. 8; 'partis vestrae homo'.
[2] He was a leader of the pagan reaction under the usurper Eugenius at Rome 392–4, and committed suicide on his downfall.
[3] At least, he was baptized on his deathbed. His character was the reverse of fanatical.
[4] *CIL* III, 9506.   [5] Theodorus; Augustine dedicated *de Vita beata* to him.
[6] Anicius Probinus, son of Sex. Petronius Probus.
[7] Generosus, the recipient of Aug. *Ep.* 116.   [8] Alfenius Ceionius Camenius.
[9] Magnilius, a connexion of Symmachus.   [10] Castorius, *CIL* IX, 5300.

governors became Christian that the laws against the Donatists began to be put into effect.[1]

The Donatists did not have to wait long to see how rapidly imperial policy could change. In 378 Valens was overwhelmed at Adrianople, and the Goths appeared outside Constantinople. To maintain unity at this crisis freedom of worship was restored to all save the Manichaeans, Eunomians and Photinians.[2] But no sooner was the situation restored and Theodosius in control than this freedom was abrogated by a fresh law[3] including in its condemnation the practice of rebaptism, peculiar to the Donatists. In spite of this, they were able to hold a council in 380 and condemn their greatest theologian, Tyconius.[4] There is not a sign of these laws being put into effect. The position of the schismatics was made even safer by the appointment of Gildo as count of Africa in 387. As commander of all the military forces there, he had greater practical authority than the civil officials. Whatever his personal beliefs, he gave support and protection to the Donatists, in particular to Optatus, bishop of Thamugadi from 388 who became notorious for his violence,[5] and who, owing to his association with the future rebel, was later abusively known as *Gildonianus*; it was commonly said of him 'comitem habet deum'. Gildo's support for the Donatists, while it protected them from the rigour of the laws against them, which could hardly be executed without the use of troops, did not go so far as to allow them to attack the Catholics outside southern Numidia, the area in which Optatus' diocese was situated.

The activity of Optatus was largely directed towards the suppression of the Maximianists, an internal division of Donatism. The Maximianists were condemned at a council at Bagai in 394 and subsequently faced with innumerable lawsuits over the restitution of their basilicas to the Donatists. That the Donatists could thus not only plead but win their cases shows how the governors, in face of the circumstances, ignored the proscriptions against them.

If Gildo was relying upon the support of the Donatists to reinforce the African army under his command, he was grievously mistaken.[6]

---

[1] *Cod. Theod.* XVI. 5. 4 (378) mentions the 'iudicum profanorum improbitas' which permitted illegal gatherings of heretics.   [2] Sozomen, *Hist. Eccl.* VII. 1.

[3] *Cod. Theod.* XVI. 5. 5 (3 August 379).   [4] Aug. *contra Epist. Parmen.* I. 1.

[5] *Contra Litt. Pet.* II. 23. 53–55, II. 83. 184, I. 24. 26, etc.

[6] Aug. *Ep.* 87. 4 says that Donatists also had suffered from the violence of Optatus and Gildo, and advises the Donatist bishop Emeritus not to descend to defending such persons.

His forces disintegrated at once before the inconsiderable army sent against him. The prosecution of the accomplices of Gildo was ordered in a series of laws promulgated between 398 and 409.[1]

A further loophole by which the Donatists could escape before pliant magistrates was given by the fact that they were not yet legally defined as heretics, and could thus plead that the various laws against heresy were not applicable to them. However, since heresy was defined as the profession of some doctrine condemned by the Church, and rebaptism was such a doctrine, the Catholics sought a judicial decision confirming that Donatism was heretical. An action was brought in 395 or 396 by the Catholics against Optatus of Thamugadi himself[2] before the vicar of Africa, doubtless without success; but in 403 the Donatist bishop of Calama was judged a heretic by the proconsul of Africa[3] and fined ten pounds of gold under a law of 392[4] inflicting such a penalty on heretical clergy. Catholic bishops were at once sent to Rome to have this decision confirmed. A comprehensive edict of 12 February 405[5] confirmed that Donatism was a heresy, ordered the application of previous laws, forbade rebaptism and the right of dissidents to make or receive legacies. There was now no legal basis on which the Donatists could hope to stand. This 'edict of unity' was at once to be published throughout Africa. A further law of the same year ordered the immediate exaction of the fines in gold from heretical clergy.[6]

These laws fixed the method of dealing with the heresy, later additions merely stimulating the authorities or varying the penalties. The Donatists were to be destroyed by the removal of their leaders— exile for the bishops[7] and heavy fines for the clergy, which if unpaid, as they must have been in many places, led to exile or imprisonment. The handing-over of basilicas and properties where meetings took place was also ordered. The laws had some degree of success and in many cases Donatist communities were entirely converted.[8] Violence was not lacking on both sides.[9] Although the heresy was far from being crushed

---

[1] E.g. *Cod. Theod.* VII. 8. 7 and 9.

[2] Aug. *contra Litt. Pet.* II. 83. 184. There were thus limits to the pressure which Gildo could apply.   [3] *Contra Cresconium*, III. 47. 51.   [4] *Cod. Theod.* XVI. 5. 21.

[5] *Cod. Theod.* XVI. 6. 4.   [6] *Cod. Theod.* XVI. 5. 39.

[7] Aug. *Ep.* 93. 1. 1; 'de multorum correctione gaudemus'. Some were *circumcelliones* (*ibid.* 1. 2).

[8] Aug. *Ep.* 93. 5. 16.   [9] Aug. *Ep.* 88. 11; 93. 12. 50. *Gesta coll. Carth.* I. 139.

—there were more Donatist than Catholic representatives at the Conference of Carthage in 411—the Catholics gained enormously and it had been shown that strong action would by no means bring the torrent of violence and bloodshed which some had perhaps feared. The laws continued to threaten, the officials were constantly urged to apply them.[1] Only for a moment was the pressure halted[2]—when it appeared that the Goths were about to invade Africa. As soon as the danger was past, Honorius sent a special commissioner to Carthage to hold a conference between the two parties and establish religious unity in the interest of the party which was vindicated. The Donatists had to obey, though the outcome was inevitable.

The laws[3] following on the condemnation of Donatism at the Conference of Carthage broke the heresy. All previous measures were confirmed and a scale of heavy fines imposed from the highest to the lowest grades of society. Special commissioners were sent from the court to supervise their execution—a significant hint of the weakness or sympathy of officials on the spot. Numerous references in Augustine[4] point to the widespread success of the measures. Although some Donatist communities still existed at the end of the sixth century, it would be an exaggeration to consider them as anything more than insignificant and isolated remnants.[5]

Some conclusions may now be drawn concerning the place of Donatism in North African social life. In the first place, it clearly did not express any deep anti-Roman feeling among the native population. Had this been the case, it would have obtained its greatest strength among the Moorish tribes in northern Numidia, the Aures, and Mauretania. However, not only did the Moors ultimately adopt Catholicism, but were in a pacific state during most of the fourth century, and later, in some cases, joined with the remaining romanized population in setting up independent kingdoms. It is true that many African cities were destroyed by natives at the end of the Vandal epoch;[6]

---

[1] *Cod. Theod.* IX. 40. 19, XVI. 5. 45, XVI. 2. 31.   [2] *Cod. Theod.* XVI. 5. 51 (410).
[3] *Cod. Theod.* XVI. 5. 52, 54 (412 and 414).
[4] Aug. *Epp.* 204. 1, 209. 2; *de Gestis cum Emerito*, 2.
[5] W. H. C. Frend, in *JRS* XXX (1940), 48, attributes some importance to the surviving Donatist communities. Yet Victor de Vita, victim and historian of the persecution of the Catholics in Africa by the Vandals, does not mention the Donatists who might have been thought to welcome such an event. In fact, there were Donatists among the refugees who fled from Africa to Gaul in the fifth century; Leo, *Ep.* 167. 18 (*PL* LIV, 1209), Avitus, *Ep.* 24 (*PL* LIX, 240).   [6] E.g. Thamugadi; Procop. *de Bell. Vand.* IV. 13. 32.

but much of this destruction was certainly due to nomad barbarians from outside the Roman provinces, and the rest may be attributed to simple desire for plunder rather than to any deep-seated national or religious hatred.

Although there are numerous instances of the strength of Donatism in various cities, it is clear that it was most powerful among the country people, the *coloni*, particularly in the villages of Numidia, and Mauretania Sitifensis. The only explicit statement about open class feeling concerns the *circumcelliones*, for whose violence there may be a special reason, namely their struggle to avoid being tied to the soil. Although the *coloni* in Proconsularis appear to have been largely Catholic, and allowing for such motives as the rural conservatism which kept the people of many Numidian sees faithful to the tradition of those who had followed Secundus of Tigisi, it seems also clear that Donatism gained some of its impetus among this class because of its attitude towards the Catholic Church which had become associated with an oppressive government. In the proconsular province, the Catholics retained possession and the initiative; the density of towns probably ensured that the people had a slightly higher standard of life than in Numidia; prosperity was less dependent on the success of a single crop or the climate: in Numidia the vast majority of the people lived in villages on the great private or imperial estates, and had little contact with urban life; exploitation by the landowners or their *conductores* was much more likely in the outlying parts, and the presence of troops imposed extra burdens on the frontier regions. There is, however, no contradiction between the conclusion that the un-romanized peasants of Numidia were enthusiastic for Donatism largely out of hatred of the government and the fact that the movement never took on a national colour. The *coloni*, though their position was hard, had little to gain by associating with nomads from the desert and the barbarians of the mountainous regions. Though all were un-romanized, their interests were conflicting.[1] Evidence for a welcome to barbarian invasions by a desperate peasantry is altogether lacking in Africa; nor were the *circumcelliones* in any way as dangerous as the Bagaudae of Gaul, who produced full-scale insurrections under Carinus and Diocletian and in later reigns.[2] Doubtless the fact that the Donatist 'Church of the Saints' was confined to

---

[1] See above, p. 26, for a similar conclusion about the relations between *limitanei* and nomads. [2] Eumen. *Paneg.* II. 4, III. 5.

Africa raised still higher the self-esteem of the African patriot; but such provincial patriotism was not confined to the schismatics.[1]

It is probable also that some of the leaders of the Donatists, belonging to or having connexions with the class of *curiales*, were likewise attracted to the schism which would express in the only way possible their resentment at the plight of their class. The political thought of this time made any expression of social protest except in the most general terms as impossible as outright nationalism (with which the Donatist leaders could never have sympathized, even had it existed). But in the scanty remains of Donatist literature we can still see those phenomena of enthusiastic self-righteousness,[2] love of personal abuse as argument,[3] and entire indifference to truth[4] which often seem to mark the union of peasant and intellectual in revolt.

The long inaction of the imperial authorities probably results from the fact that the benefits to be gained from the suppression of Donatism were not sufficient to outweigh the trouble. The reasons for Constantine's refusal to take further action after 322 have already been noted. In general the strictly local problem was far overshadowed by the Arian controversy which involved the whole Empire and the court itself. That the schism could be driven underground with only a moderate use of force was shown in 347, though the success of Macarius was not pursued as the revival under Julian showed. Relatively untroubled by barbarians, the function of Africa was to serve as a granary for Italy. So long as there was no interruption in the collection of the *annona* or collaboration with disturbers of the peace and public enemies, the emperors were prepared to allow a surprising amount of freedom in religious differences. Africa was, besides, out of the main stream of imperial politics; there was no group of high officials or ecclesiastics of African origin[5] at court who might influence the emperor to intervene.

This fact becomes the more evident when we consider that it was only after the implication of some Donatists in a long and difficult rebellion that Gratian abandoned the policy of his predecessors. From

---

[1] See below, p. 105.   [2] Cf. *Acta Saturnini*, 20 (*PL* VIII, 703).

[3] E.g. Optatus, III. 3; Donatus to the praetorian prefect Gregorius, 'macula senatus et dedecus praefectorum'. Cf. also the sentence of the council of Bagai (394) against the Maximianists; Aug. *de Gestis cum Emerito*, 10 (*PL* XI, 1190).

[4] They never accepted (nor, of course, could they) the innocence of Felix of Apthungi.

[5] See below, pp. 106 f.

the time of the suppression of Firmus the emperors cannot be charged with weakness so far as their intention goes; with only two interruptions in times of extreme crisis the series of repressive laws continued. Both Theodosius and Honorius had few scruples about the use of secular power in the interests of orthodoxy. What delayed the downfall of the Donatists was the attitude of the governors, officials, and landowners. Reasons for this have already been given—the continued paganism of the majority, the possibility of changes in policy which might ruin an enthusiastic governor. Active execution of the laws might also bring local disorders which could be injurious to a career. Besides, there were substantial and respected citizens in every community who adhered to Donatism and were prepared to use every legal method in its defence; the Donatist Church was wealthy and could afford apparently endless lawsuits and appeals. Finally, there were the landowners with their personal power, who were mostly pagan or Catholic, but who hindered every attempt by the officials to intervene on their estates. Such was their determination in this respect that Augustine, writing about 401, though hoping that other Christian landowners would now follow the example of his friend Pammachius in applying pressure to their Donatist *coloni* said it was actually dangerous to mention the subject to them.[1] The execution of the anti-Donatist laws was, in fact, an impossibility without their co-operation. This was recognized by the authorities,[2] but even so enthusiastic a Catholic as St Melania still had a Donatist bishop on her estate near Thagaste in 410.[3]

Augustine's incessant efforts begun in 392 for the complete victory of Catholicism in Africa were, perhaps, the decisive factor. At the time of his first intervention, the Donatists were still strong in the legal anomalies and the attitude of governors and landowners which prevented the full application of the laws. Augustine, besides a vast amount of polemical literature against Donatism, wrote numerous letters encouraging governors and landowners to use all their powers to crush the schism. His influence grew every year; he was in contact with some of the most powerful men of the time. He provided the Catholics with the leadership which had been lacking for so long, and played a large part in the final defeat of Donatism.

[1] Aug. *Ep.* 58. 3; 'illos periculosum est exhortari'.
[2] *Cod. Theod.* XVI. 2. 31 (398).   [3] *Vita S. Mel.* 21.

CHAPTER VIII

INTELLECTUAL LIFE

THE intellectual leadership of the Western half of the Empire which Africa had held in the second and third centuries went during the fourth to Gaul.[1] Africa had no counterpart of the culture which flourished in Aquitaine, and which is described by Ausonius. Yet there are sufficient remains, particularly in the fields of grammar and rhetoric, to indicate the enthusiasm which the upper classes still retained for the maintenance of culture.

In the first place, the traditional education continued to be given in the schools which any city worthy of the name still maintained. Throughout this century the *rhetores* and *grammatici* of both Greek and Latin, who had charge of the system, were treated as a privileged class and freed from the municipal burdens to which their wealth should have bound them.[2] As many of the cities through poverty or sheer disinclination began to reduce the salaries, these were later fixed by the state.[3] The law of Gratian which enacted this was almost certainly issued at the suggestion of the emperor's former tutor, Ausonius, the most distinguished poet of his time. Although we have no such testimony to the African teachers as Ausonius provides for those of Bordeaux,[4] there is no doubt that they were numerous and often of a high standard. St Augustine received a grounding at his native Thagaste, a small town in Proconsularis near the borders of Numidia; he himself taught there for a short time as a *grammaticus* at the outset of his career. Though he was taught Greek, as he tells us in a well-known passage,[5] he never made much progress. The important fact, however, is that, though a knowledge of Greek was becoming rare all over the Western Empire at this time, even in lettered circles,[6] it was taught in even this small provincial town in Africa. Augustine afterwards went for more advanced study to Madauros. This city had been

---

[1] Cf. Thieling, *Der Hellenismus in Kleinafrika*, 175.
[2] *Cod. Theod.* XIII. 3. 1–3 from the reign of Constantine.
[3] *Cod. Theod.* XIII. 3. 11 (376); '…oratoribus viginti quattuor annonarum e fisco emolumenta donentur…etc.'
[4] Ausonius, *de Prof. Burd.* See also Haarhof, *The Schools of Gaul, passim.*
[5] *Confess.* I. 13. 20 and I. 14. 23.   [6] Thieling, *op. cit.* 161.

a considerable centre of Roman culture ever since the time of its most famous citizen Apuleius. We may note the number of inscriptions in verse, including some epitaphs from the fourth century to Christians;[1] they make up a high proportion of such inscriptions in the case of Africa. At the end of the century a local grammarian, Maximus, expressed sentiments against Christianity which are very similar to those of the highest pagan society in Rome.[2] Yet Madauros was a small city compared with many in North Africa, and was isolated from the main roads. The education of many of Augustine's Donatist opponents shows that other cities also were not lacking in schools. Far superior to all these, however, was Carthage. Not only was it easily the most important African city in every way; it was second only to Rome as a centre for Latin studies, as Augustine mentioned when writing to a wealthy Greek who had come there to study the Latin language and literature.[3] The number of teachers was immense, and most of the famous African men of letters had lived or studied there for some length of time. Augustine was enabled to continue his studies at Carthage through the help of a wealthy friend. Later he himself taught rhetoric there, becoming friendly with the proconsul Vindicianus and winning a prize in a public contest. The students at Carthage were too violent for his liking, however, and he left the city for Rome.[4] Educated society at Carthage with which Augustine came into contact was often augmented by the arrival of a proconsul or vicar with literary tastes. The most eminent of these in the fourth century was undoubtedly the orator Symmachus (*Procos. Afr.* 371–3); another important figure was the historian Nicomachus Flavianus (vicar of Africa, 376–7); Augustine's friend Vindicianus was a very eminent doctor. Arnobius, writing at the beginning of the century, probably saw performed at Carthage not only the usual farces and mimes but plays of Sophocles, Euripides and Plautus.[5] The addiction of the people of this city to the pleasures of the circus and the theatre even when the Vandals were threatening was a scandal to severer minds.[6]

The majority of the African writers whose works have survived were

---

[1] E.g. *ILAlg* 2195, 2209, 2221, 2240, etc. (pagan); 2768–77 (Christian).

[2] See his letter, Aug. *Ep.* 16; and Augustine's reply, *Ep.* 17.

[3] Aug. *Ep.* 118; 'duae tantae urbes Latinarum litterarum artifices Roma et Carthago'. See also Salvian, *de Gub. Dei*, VII. 67 f.

[4] Aug. *Confess.* IV. 3. 5, V. 8. 14; *Ep.* 138. 3.

[5] Arnob. IV. 35, VII. 33.   [6] Salvian, *de Gub. Dei*, VI. 69.

themselves teachers by profession. Arnobius was a professor of rhetoric in the city of Veneria Sicca in Africa Proconsularis during the reign of Diocletian. In his early life, his paganism had not only been of the philosophic nature common to the educated class of the time, but expressed itself in a devotion to traditional rites. His conversion to Christianity during the reign of Diocletian shows him to have been a man of considerable courage.

Arnobius seems never to have left Africa. His more famous pupil Lactantius followed a different career. He too was an African, possibly from Cirta.[1] His reputation was soon so considerable that he, with another African, Flavius a *grammaticus*, was called by Diocletian to Nicomedia, then the capital city in the eastern part of the Empire.[2] This position came to an end with the great persecution. Between 313 and 318 Lactantius moved to Constantine's domain and became tutor to the emperor's son Crispus. Like his teacher Lactantius had been at first a pagan; the circumstances of his conversion are obscure; it may well have taken place before he left Africa. Here the resemblance between the two ends. In the style and tone of his apologetical works, 'Lactance est d'ordinaire aussi paisible et calme qu'Arnobe était nerveux et agité.'[3] The *Adversus nationes* of Arnobius was an apology, written to convince those doubtful of the genuineness of his conversion,[4] while Lactantius with a wider and more cultivated audience in view, and the persecutions apparently finished for ever, wrote his later work as a moralist and Christian humanist.[5] Both Arnobius and Lactantius show some antipathy to Rome as the source of paganism and persecution, and it is also possible that they were influenced by regional patriotism which in Africa manifested itself in pride at the long defiance of the Carthaginians against the armies of the Republic.[6]

It is beyond the scope and purpose of this work to attempt any estimate of Augustine, with his overwhelming pre-eminence in the intellectual life at the end of the Western Empire. It may, however, be noted that only a very few years of his life were spent outside Africa; from this we may deduce that the intellectual resources of the province

---

[1] *C* 7241 refers to L. Caecilius Firmianus, undoubtedly a relative of the writer, whose full name seems to have been L. Caecilius Firmianus qui et Lactantius.

[2] Jer. *de Vir. ill.* 80.   [3] Gilson, *La Philosophie au moyen âge*, 106.

[4] Jer. *Chron. ad ann.* 2343.

[5] See Jer. *Ep.* xxxv for the comments of Pope Damasus on Lactantius' lack of doctrine.

[6] See Arnob. I. 5, VII. 47; Lactant. *Divin. inst.* VII. 5, VII. 11 f.

were sufficient for him in his youth (he did not leave Africa till some years after he had completed his education); and that in later life contact between Africa and other centres such as Rome, Milan and the East was good enough for Augustine to keep fully informed of intellectual and theological developments.

Other products of the African schools of the fourth century may be briefly mentioned. Marius Victorinus, who was certainly born and brought up in Africa, went to Rome about 340 and opened a school of rhetoric. This rapidly became the most fashionable in the city and Victorinus was honoured by a statue in the forum. His conversion in 355 created a sensation, as he had long been a powerful antagonist of Christianity.[1] Through his adoption of Neo-platonism, Victorinus is of importance in the history of philosophy, for he influenced St Augustine in this direction.[2] An almost exact contemporary was the grammarian Charistus who became a professor at Constantinople in 358. Appointments of this sort at the capital were usually dependent on the agreement of the emperor; the reputation of Charistus must have been considerable even before he left Africa. It is quite possible that he is to be identified with the pagan grammarian Charisius.[3] We have brief references to other literary figures at the end of the fourth century. Favonius Eulogius was taught by Augustine at Carthage about 385; he was a specialist on Cicero, and seems to have lived somewhere in Byzacena.[4] Tullius Marcellus of Carthage was the author of a popular philosophical hand-book praised by Cassiodorus.[5] These were probably pagan; but Fonteius, an ethical writer from Carthage, became a Christian at the end of his life.[6]

It may be noted that in spite of the education evidently available in Africa, the number of men from that province who became prominent in the history of the fourth century is very small. It is known that many of the surviving middle classes entered the staffs of the vicar, the count, the provincial governors and other high officials.[7] But in these highest

---

[1] Jer. de Vir. ill. 101.

[2] Gilson, op. cit. 125; Aug. Confess. VIII. 2. 3.

[3] Jer. Chron. ad ann. 2375=358. See also Teuffel and Schwabe, History of Roman Literature, II, 360.

[4] See Cicero (ed. Orelli), v. 397–407; Aug. de Cura pro mortuis agenda II. 13 (CSEL XLI, 642. 12).

[5] Cassiod. de Artibus ac disciplinis liberalium litterarum, III (PL LXX, 1173).

[6] Aug. de divers. Quaest. XII (PL XL, 14); Retract. I. 26 (PL XXXII, 624).

[7] Cf. the Album of Thamugadi, which records sons of curiales in officia.

positions Gauls, Pannonians, and the city aristocracy provided the vast majority of the civil appointments while Germans gradually became supreme in military posts. Ammianus Marcellinus in his very detailed account of the years 353–78 mentions only two Africans who became prominent: Eupraxius, from Mauretania Caesariensis, *magister memoriae* in 367,[1] who is recorded as having been a man of fearless justice, and the historian Aurelius Victor who was born in Tripolitania, governed Pannonia Inferior under Julian and became prefect in the city in 388/9.[2] Doubtless there were others; at the beginning of the fifth century two of the proconsuls of Africa were natives of the province.[3] But there is no doubt that in general Africans were conspicuous by their absence from positions of influence. Yet in the second century, Africans had been second only to Spaniards in their importance in the administration, and at the beginning of the third were the dominant western provincial group. It was the anarchy of the latter part of the third century that made a public career distasteful to the educated class in the more advanced parts of the Empire. Not only did the urban aristocracy suffer terribly at the hands of peasant emperors and soldiers, but the noble and the wealthy found it preferable to avoid public life and live on their estates. At the same time parts of the Empire which had formerly been unimportant, especially the Balkan provinces, became the chief centres of power because, in so far as the military strength of the Empire still came from within its borders, it came from those provinces.

When stability was restored by Diocletian and his successors, the senate as it had been at the end of the second century no longer existed. There was, indeed, a new upper class which had gained power and wealth by various means during the years of chaos. Those of its number who took an active part in affairs mostly came from those parts of the Empire which had lately risen to prominence. The aristocracy in the African provinces, now no longer influential, remained to a large extent in political obscurity—and material prosperity, if our estimate of the wealth of Africa as late as the fifth century is correct. It is also worth remarking that the Africans who had gone to Rome in the second century and later were rapidly absorbed into the city aristocracy. Such was the end of the Antistii, related to M. Aurelius,

---

[1] Amm. Marc. XXVII. 6. 14.
[2] Amm. Marc. XXI. 10. 6; praised by Ammianus as 'sobrietatis gratia aemulandus'.
[3] Donatus (408), Celer (427).

and the family of the orator Cornelius Fronto. One of the protagonists in the *Octavius* of Minucius Felix, the Christian apologist, writing in the first half of the third century, is represented as living in Rome, though his birthplace was Cirta.[1] The only powerful families of the fourth century who had an African origin were the Caecinae Albini and the much less eminent Aradii. Neither of these appear before the closing years of the third century, and the Ceionii soon became connected with the highest society in Rome being prolific and cautious enough to survive the end of the Western Empire.[2] It may be observed that a lack of enterprise and ambition also affected the African Catholics who after Cyprian showed scarcely a sign of intellectual vigour either in Africa or at court till the time of Augustine.

The upper class in Africa thus consisted of wealthy landowners mostly living on their estates and taking little part in public affairs. The religious outlook and personality of some are revealed to us through the letters of Augustine. The saint, in his African correspondence, not only engaged in controversies with the Donatists and stimulated governors to effective action against heretics, but also discussed religion with wealthy pagans of the province and advised Catholic nobles in matters of conscience.

Of his pagan correspondents in Africa, the most eminent was Volusianus. He was the elder son of Publilius Ceionius Caecina Albinus, and had been *comes rei privatae* in 408. The letters between Volusianus and Augustine are dated to 412;[3] it seems likely that he had taken up residence in Carthage after the sack of Rome by the Goths, as had many other wealthy Romans—though Volusianus had the advantage of a family connexion with Africa. Volusianus was a pagan, though the son of a Christian mother, and used to discuss Christianity with Marcellinus, the commissioner sent to settle the Donatist question in 411, through whom he exchanged views with Augustine. Another pagan of philosophic views who appears in the letters was Longinianus,[4] who had held certain priesthoods and who had (like all Augustine's pagan friends) the greatest regard for the bishop. Lastly, mention may be made of a certain Rusticus, who had the rank of *vir spectabilis*. Augustine would not permit a young girl in the care of the Church to marry Rusticus' son who was still a pagan.[5] Paganism at Carthage was

---

[1] *Octavius*, 9. 6.   [2] See the stemma in *P-W* III, 1862.
[3] Aug. *Epp.* 135, 137, 138.   [4] Aug. *Epp.* 233-5.   [5] *Ep.* 252.

very strong; in 399 the temple of Dea Caelestis, the most revered deity of the city, was shut on imperial instructions, but popular unrest and demonstrations at the place were such that it was levelled to the ground in 421.[1]

Some of the Christian correspondents of Augustine were equally prominent. He addressed one letter[2] to Pammachius, the wealthy Roman senator and friend of St Jerome. Pammachius may have been at one time proconsul of Africa;[3] at any rate he had large estates in Numidia, and though living so far away had obliged his *coloni* to renounce Donatism. This action was highly praised by Augustine. Similarly, Festus, who held some kind of public office, had sent a letter to his *coloni* near Hippo Regius requiring them to give up Donatism. This had been ineffective and Augustine suggested that Festus should send a friend or a servant to him for advice on how to proceed further.[4]

Valerius Publicola, father of St Melania, who had estates on the frontier near the boundary between Byzacena and Tripolitania, required to be reassured that contracts made with barbarian pagans were not sinful.[5] Nebridius, a wealthy citizen of Carthage with estates near the city, had a passion for discussing most obscure points of doctrine and exchanged many letters with Augustine.[6] There was further a certain Celer, who was proconsul of Africa[7] at the very end of Roman rule. This man, with an estate near Hippo Regius, had previously been a Donatist,[8] and Augustine was instrumental in persuading him to give up the heresy and to apply pressure to his *coloni* to do the same. Another African, Donatus, who was proconsul in 408 was also asked by Augustine to further the Catholic cause among his men near Hippo Regius.[9] Last of all may be mentioned the name of Anicia Faltonia Proba: the daughter of Clodius Hermogenianus Olybrius (proconsul of Africa in 361), widow of Sex. Petronius Probus (proconsul of Africa in 358), the mother of three consuls, she was from the wealthiest and most powerful family in the Empire. After the sack of Rome by the Goths she went to Africa with a company of Roman noblewomen

---

[1] *Liber de promissionibus Dei*, III. 44.   [2] *Ep.* 58 (beginning of 401).
[3] Pallu de Lessert, *op. cit.* II, 143.   [4] *Ep.* 89 (about 406).
[5] *Epp.* 45, 46.
[6] *Epp.* 3–14 (after 388). He had attached himself to Augustine when the latter was teaching at Carthage.
[7] *Cod. Theod.* XII. 1. 185 (429).   [8] *Epp.* 56, 57 (c. 400).
[9] *Ep.* 113 (408).

and led a semi-conventual life with them. Her granddaughter Demetrias became a nun about this time and received a famous letter from St Jerome.[1] Augustine, in a letter to Proba, favourably compared the merit of being the ancestor of Demetrias with that of bearing three consuls.

The lay society with which Augustine was in contact was thus one of wealth and education. The division in this class between over-scrupulous Christians and conservative pagans was similar to that in other parts of the West. The capture of Rome by the Goths and the devastations in Italy had brought an influx of refugees, no doubt largely from the upper classes in Italy. This doubtless increased the strength of the Catholics in the African provinces. Proba, who brought a whole retinue of noblewomen, and Melania, who though not in flight from the Goths arrived in Africa at the same time, were but the most eminent of those who brought an enthusiasm for the convent. Despite the interest of St Augustine in this movement, the African Catholics had been too occupied in fighting the Donatists for it to become wide-spread. In fact, as late as 385, there were probably extremely few monastic establishments in Africa; for at that date Augustine himself was entirely ignorant of the institution.[2] According to Salvian, the Africans of the last years before the Vandal conquest were hostile to the monks,[3] and there can be little doubt that it was owing to the wealthy refugees that there were so many religious houses at that time. Heresies apart from Donatism do not seem to have flourished in Africa outside Carthage. The Africans were not much given to theological speculation, and the prominence of heretical sects at Carthage was doubtless due to the number of immigrants from other provinces who were attracted to the great port and university city. There was a substantial colony of Greeks at all times, and among these were doubt-less the Manichaeans whom Diocletian ordered to be suppressed in 296.[4] They were, of course, still existing at the end of the fourth century when Augustine joined them for some years, and were per-secuted by the Vandals still later.[5] Pelagius and his chief disciple Celestius visited Carthage in 411/12, and it was there that their opinions

[1] *Ep.* 22.

[2] Aug. *Confess.* VIII. 6; cf. Leclercq, *Dict. d'arch. chrét.*, s.v. cénobitisme, 3225 f.

[3] *De Gub. Dei*, VIII. 24.

[4] See W. Seston, 'Achilleus et la révolte de l'Égypte sous Dioclétien', *Mél. arch. et hist.* LIV (1938), 184.   [5] Victor de Vita, II. 1.

first aroused the suspicions of the Catholic episcopate. They do not, however, seem to have found any support in Africa. Arianism had never gained a foothold, but at the very end of Roman rule we hear of Arians at Hippo Regius[1] and Carthage[2] whom Augustine thought it worth while to combat. These undoubtedly came with the Gothic troops who now comprised a major part of the African army, or from Ravenna where the court was equally under German influence.

Though the upper class in Africa retained much of its culture to the end, there can be no denying that the original products of Africa were meagre in the extreme—no Ausonius, no Claudian, no Prudentius to enliven their dull pedantry. The tradition of the African grammarians was so strong that it survived the Vandal invasions. Several names[3] including that of Priscian from Caesarea are recorded as having continued it in Africa or Constantinople. But the last great figure of pagan Africa before the Vandal conquest, Martianus Capella of Madauros, epitomizes the African literary tendencies of the time: 'Mélange de prose et de vers, d'érudition indigeste et de fantaisie, de négligence et de raffinement pittoresque, de façons populaires et de stylisme....'[4] We have arrived at the Middle Ages. Martianus' 'De nuptiis Philologiae et Mercurii', the object of the above criticism, was one of the most influential books in Western Europe during the next ten centuries.[5]

[1] Possidius, *Vita Aug.* 17; Maximinus, an Arian bishop.
[2] Possidius, *ibid.*; Aug. *Ep.* 238; Pascentius, *comes domus regiae* and described as *fisci vehementissimus exactor.*
[3] Thieling, *op. cit.* 164 and 165.   [4] Monceaux, *Les Africains,* 445.
[5] *P-W* XIV, 2012, 2013.

EPILOGUE

The Conference of 411 was the last major event in North African history before the Vandal Conquest. The first quarter of the fifth century in North Africa is one of peculiar calm and quiet[1] compared with the torrents of ruin falling upon the rest of Western Europe. An attempt in 413 by Heraclian, *comes Africae*, to take advantage of the chaos in the West was as quickly crushed as that of Gildo; that is all the political history of the time. The names of the governors, if known, are obscure; the urban class has perished; the Donatists submit with only sporadic outbursts to the combined pressure of officials and land-owners. The only signs of activity of any form were at Hippo, whence Augustine continued to pour out an unbelievable number of tracts and letters addressed to the Christians in all parts of the dying Empire. His meditations upon that immense catastrophe were, moreover, being embodied in the composition of his greatest work. He can have had little doubt about the eventual fate of his home in one form of disaster or another long before the Vandals appeared under the walls of Hippo. He had long since commented bitterly on the fact that throughout the Empire peace and security rested solely on the oaths of pagans and barbarians.[2]

Save for the sea-crossing, the Vandals had an easy task. The armed opposition was feeble in the extreme; only some cities held out for a while behind their powerful fortifications. The *limitanei* were trained to fight marauders from the desert, not the migration of a whole people. The mass of the peasants might view without much interest the sack of their lord's villa and his replacement by a Vandal *chiliarch*. The wealthy fled, if they could, to Italy and Gaul, whence many had once fled to Africa from the Goths, now shown to be a milder race than the Vandals.

Africa was never visited by a Roman emperor after Maximian (298); it was, as it were, a military backwater. Nor did the disturbances

---

[1] Victor de Vita (1. 2) says that the Vandals found Africa 'pacatam quietamque provinciam speciositatem totius terrae florentis'.

[2] Aug. *Ep.* 46.

occasioned by the Donatist schism give sufficient cause for personal intervention by the emperor. The *annona civica* was never interrupted save by the usurpers at the end of the century. In an economy thus unaffected by serious devastation from wars, it becomes clear that the real crisis took place in the years after the death of Gratian. Up to that time, owing to the natural wealth of the land and the palliative measures of Valentinian, the *curiales* had survived, and were even, for a while, prosperous. In the last years of Roman rule in Africa, a rapid decline is shown by the flight of *curiales* to positions lower in society, by the increasing power of the great landowners, and the inability of the central power to curb the exactions of the officials. These problems had, of course, been known through the century, but they became insuperable in its last two decades. A final point worth stressing arises from the evidence put forward in this essay; it is further confirmation of the greatness of Valentinian. He has rightly been honoured for his defence of the Rhine frontier against continued attack, and his zeal for the protection of the people against their official or senatorial oppressors. From the African evidence it is clear that his positive measures for the relief of the *curiales* had a real, if temporary, success. This confirms the judgement of Ammianus, who in general is severe towards him: 'he was very indulgent towards the provincials and everywhere lightened the burden of their tributes.'[1] After his death, though the religious controversy was certainly exhausting and administrative pressure everywhere was made worse by the crisis of 378, the rapid decline of Africa, a region immune from devastation by the barbarians, indicates how overwhelming were the difficulties faced by his unfortunate successors.

[1] xxx. 9; Ammianus, as a contemporary of Valentinian and a man of curial origin, cannot be in error here. The opposite verdict of Zosimus (*Hist.* IV. 16) is to be rejected.

BIBLIOGRAPHY

The following is a list of the more important works on Roman North Africa and of others containing references to the subject of this book.

ALBERTINI, E. *L'Afrique romaine*. Algiers, 1932.

ALFOLDI, A. *The Conversion of Constantine and Pagan Rome*. Oxford, 1948.

BARADEZ, J. *Fossatum Africae*. Paris, 1949.

BARTHEL, W. *Zur Geschichte der römischen Städte in Africa*. Greifswald, 1904.

BAYNES, N. H. 'Constantine the Great and the Christian Church', in *Proceedings of the British Academy*, vol. XV, 1929.

BERTHIER, A. *Les Vestiges du christianisme dans la Numidie antique*. Algiers, 1943.

BROUGHTON, T. R. S. *The Romanization of Africa Proconsularis*. Baltimore, 1929.

CAGNAT, R. *L'Armée romaine d'Afrique*. Paris, 1912.

CARCOPINO, J. *Le Maroc antique*. Paris, 1943.

DIEHL, CH. *L'Afrique byzantine*. Paris, 1896.

DILL, S. *Roman Society in the Last Century of the Western Empire*. London, 1899.

DUCHESNE, L. 'Le dossier du donatisme', in *Mélanges de l'École française*, 1890.

FREND, W. H. C. *The Donatist Church—a Movement of Protest in Roman North Africa*. Oxford, 1952.

GAUCKLER, P. *Enquête sur les installations hydrauliques romaines en Tunisie*. Tunis, 1897.

GAUTIER, E. F. *Les Siècles obscures du Maghreb*. Paris, 1927.

GSELL, S. *Atlas archéologique de l'Algérie*. Paris, 1902–11.

GSELL, S. *Les Monuments antiques de l'Algérie*. Paris, 1901.

GSELL et JOLY. *Khamissa, Mdaourouch, Announa*. Paris, 1914–22.

JULIEN, CH.-A. *Histoire de l'Afrique du Nord* (with extensive bibliography of sources and studies on all periods of North African history). Paris, 1931.

LOT, F. *La Fin du monde antique*. Paris, 1927.

MARTROYE, F. 'La répression du donatisme', in *Mémoires de la Société des antiquaires de France*, vol. LXXIII, 1914.

MARTROYE, F. *Genséric*. Paris, 1907.

MAURICE, J. *Numismatique constantinienne*. Paris, 1908–12.

MESNAGE. *L'Afrique chrétienne*. Paris, 1912.

MONCEAUX, P. *Les Africains*. Paris, 1894.

MONCEAUX, P. *Histoire littéraire de l'Afrique chrétienne*. Paris, 1901–22.

VAN NOSTRAND, J. J. *The Imperial Domains of Africa Proconsularis*.

PALLU DE LESSERT. *Fastes des provinces africaines*. Paris, 1896.

PIGANIOL, A. *L'Empire chrétien*. Paris, 1947.

ROSTOVTZEFF, M. *Social and Economic History of the Roman Empire*. Oxford, 1926.

SCHMIDT, L. *Geschichte der Wandalen*. Leipzig, 1901.

SEECK, O. *Geschichte des Untergangs der antiken Welt*. Stuttgart, 1921.

SESTON, W. *Dioclétien et la tétrarchie*. Paris, 1946.

SHERWIN-WHITE, A. N. *The Roman Citizenship*. Oxford, 1939.

STEIN, E. *Geschichte des spätrömischen Reiches*, I. Vienna, 1928.

THIELING, W. *Der Hellenismus in Kleinafrika*. Leipzig, 1911.

THUMMEL, W. *Zur Beurteilung des Donatismus*. Halle, 1893.

TOUTAIN, J. *Les Cités romaines de la Tunisie*. Paris, 1895.

8-2

ADDITIONAL BIBLIOGRAPHY

BROWN, P. R. L. *Augustine of Hippo*. London, 1967.

BRISSON, J.-P. *Autonomisme et christianisme dans l'Afrique romaine*. Paris, 1958.

COURCELLE, P. *Histoire littéraire des grandes invasions germaniques* (3rd edition). Paris, 1965.

COURTOIS, Chr. *Les Vandales et l'Afrique*. Paris, 1955.

DIESNER, H. J. *Der Untergang der römischen Herrschaft in Nordafrika*. Weimar, 1964.

FREND, W. H. C. *Martyrdom and Persecution in the Early Church*. Oxford, 1965.

GAUDEMET, J. *L'Église dans l'Empire romain*. Paris, 1958.

HARMAND, L. *Le Patronat sur les collectivités publiques des origines au Bas-Empire*. Paris, 1957.

JONES, A. H. M. The Later Roman Empire. Oxford, 1964.

MACMULLEN, R. *Enemies of the Roman Order*. Harvard, 1967.

MAREC, E. *Monuments chrétiens d' Hippone*. Paris, 1954.

MUSSET, L. *Les Invasions—les vagues germaniques*. Paris, 1965.

PICARD, G. Ch. *La Carthage de Saint Augustin*. Paris, 1965.

PICARD, G. Ch. *La Civilisation de l'Afrique romaine*. Paris, 1959.

ROMANELLI, P. *Storia delle province Romane dell'Africa*. Rome, 1959.

TENGSTRÖM, E. *Donatisten und Katholiken: soziale, wirtschaftliche und politische Aspekte einer nordafrikanischen Kirchenspaltung*. Gothenburg, 1964.

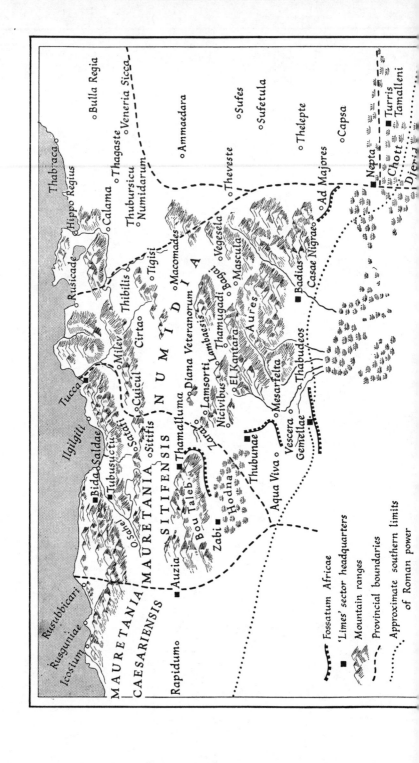

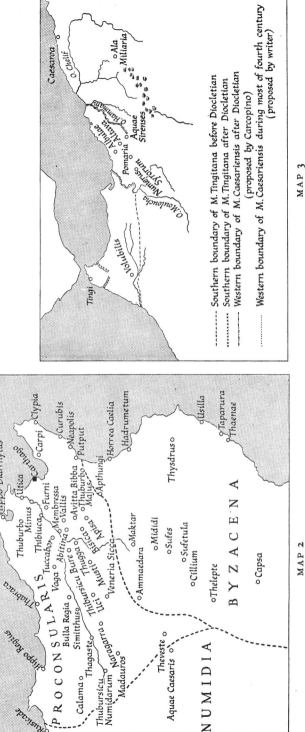

MAP 3

Southern boundary of M.Tingitana before Diocletian

---- Southern boundary of M.Tingitana after Diocletian

········· Western boundary of M.Caesariensis after Diocletian (proposed by Carcopino)

---- Western boundary of M.Caesariensis during most of fourth century (proposed by writer)

Caesarea

O.Cheliff

Ala Miliaria

Aquae Sirenses

O.Hammam

Albulae

Ad Atlas

Pomaria

Numerus Syrorum

O.Mouloucha

Volubilis

Tingi

MAP 2

Hippo Diarrhytus

Thibraca

Hippo Regius

Rusicade

Calama

Thagaste

Thubursicu Numidarum

Naragarra

Madauros

Theveste

Aquae Caesaris

N U M I D I A

P R O C O N S U L A R I S

Thuburbo Minus

Thibiuca

Utica

Carthago

Carpi

Clypia

Curubis

Neapolis

Putput

Furni

Membressa

Vallis

Avitta Bibba

Thuburbo Majus

Apthungi

Horrea Caelia

Hadrumetum

Bulla Regia

Simitthus

Thibursicu Bure

Vaga

Thugga

Abitina

Mustis

Bisica

Apisa

Uci

Veneria Sicca

Ammaedara

Maktar

Mididi

Sufes

Sufetula

Thelepte

Cillium

Capsa

B Y Z A C E N A

Thysdrus

Usilla

Taparura

Thaenae

INDEX

121